THE BEST
AUSTRALIAN
POEMS
2 0 1 1

THE BEST
AUSTRALIAN
POEMS
2011

Edited by

JOHN TRANTER

Black Inc.

Published by Black Inc.,
an imprint of Schwartz Media Pty Ltd
37–39 Langridge Street
Collingwood VIC 3066 Australia
email: enquiries@blackincbooks.com
http://www.blackincbooks.com

ISBN 9781863955492

Printed in Australia by Griffin Press. The paper this book is printed on
is certified against the Forest Stewardship Council® Standards.
Griffin Press holds FSC chain of custody certification SGS-COC-005088.
FSC promotes environmentally responsible, socially beneficial
and economically viable management of the world's forests.

FSC
www.fsc.org
MIX
Paper from
responsible sources
FSC® C009448

Contents

Introduction

EACH YEAR (SINCE 2003) BLACK INC. HAS ASKED
Australian poets to submit a selection of their work for
this anthology. This year it was my turn to read through
the two or three thousand poems that were sent in and choose
the best.

I'm not sure that we can trust the word 'best' when we're talk-
ing about poetry – there are so many different kinds of poetry,
from Homer to rock and roll, and then there are millions of
readers with their individual tastes and prejudices – but in any
case I chose a little over a hundred of what I felt were the most
vigorous, varied and interesting poems for this book.

And any honest anthologist should offer a further disclaimer:
though I have tried to be widely representative, of course I have
my own blind spots and may have failed to recognise wonderful
work; some poets may have missed the deadline for any of a
dozen reasons, some may have chosen not to offer poems to an
anthology claiming to showcase 'the best' (this has happened),
some of our best poets may have had no 'best' poems this year
but may have next year, and so forth. As different editors publish
their choices from year to year, any personal bias or imbalances
should be cancelled out.

But what a rich, strange and diverse lot these poems turned
out to be. Look at this list below, a gathering of some of the
brightest images, transformations and unbelievable events that
litter this collection. I suspect that these baroque and potent
imaginings can only have come into existence as fragments of
dreams or nightmares:

Bent hot-dogs talk to strangers. Still, the oak trees flower above us, a canopy of lust; an academic scholar talks about whoring his mind, a poetry editor apologises for not accepting a sentimental poem about a lost ant, a well-known fiction writer snoozes on the sofa, an empty brandy bottle in her lap, Boofhead's Egyptian style of ambulation and a vast mural of Fred and Wilma are discussed, mothers wonder how tiger snakes got into the linen cupboards, an unknown baby skeleton, a word in Arabic that means a tree that befriends doomed travellers, the irony of green rain, the devil on holiday in Tasmania, Picasso's one red eye, Ezra Pound's brilliant rottenness, the Master of Stomachs, a skyscraper as a babel of crockery, dawn as the clock-face of the heavens, the feedback loop of amazing grace and dead birds, phantoms on the home stretch, a woman who's doing the accounts with one hand and killing a snake with another while she gets an armful of wood, Rupert Bunny's women waiting for a take-away pizza, two shopping bags full of stuffed bears etc, a shop where dresses were hanging like marked-down lungs, an apoplectic monkey and a monkey who practises sermons too green to transcribe, gods crawling through trumpets to get here, a miracle on Blue Mouse Street (in Dublin, of course), a wolf sack filled with of courses, perhapses, and maybe, the boots of Nazis misunderstanding stairs, God smoking a pipe, love like police presence, History with its morphine headache, a new neighbour swathed in her pet python, a man who looks forward to looking back on this moment, a mincing lion and an indignant unicorn and a dragon wind, a convention of lapidarists, a gluey saraband, murder at the poetry conference, a man with echidna gloves, a love that is an inscrutable monster, tickets to the monster trucks, a beer-drinking pig, a holidaying tycoon who has popped an artery on a sodden golf course, human beings as the tennis-balls of the stars, the memorable vanilla windows of Miss Moore, a Jungian bus trip and an absinthe sea.

The American poet John Ashbery is one of the most widely read and intelligent people in the world of writing. He has thought deeply about what it means to create poems, and in an address to the Poetry Society of America in 1995, he said:

> Every poet who reads his or her poetry before an audience is accustomed to the question and answer period that follows, which often ends with the question, 'Are there any questions that haven't been asked that you feel you would like to answer?' The underlying thrust of all these questions is something like: 'Please explain your poetry to me.' Now it may be true that composers and painters and cineastes are also asked to explain their work, but if so their task is lightened somewhat by the fact that there is something there to explain. With a poem there is nothing, or there should be nothing if the poet has done his job successfully, and that is because the act of writing the poem was an explanation of something that had occurred to the poet, and demanded to be put into words which in turn formed a poem. To explain an explanation is a much more difficult, and in the end perhaps a hopeless task because it's doomed to redundancy. Yet I'm fully aware that I'll have to go on making repeated stabs at it for as long as I'll be asked to speak in public, and that this impossible feat is also a necessary one if only because people expect it, and it is normal and proper to give people what they expect.

As he suggests, there's not much point in trying to explain how poems work or what they 'mean'. But as with public talks, so with anthologies of poetry: readers expect an Introduction that will explain each of the poems, or if not that, then explain why they should bother reading all this stuff, which means 'Please explain why poetry matters.' If you're reading this page, you have the anthology in your hands, so you already have some suspicion as to why poetry might matter – matter to you, at any rate. So thank you.

But what kind of meaning do I think poems have? After all, I've written more than a thousand of them over the last half-century: I should have some idea.

Well, to be frank, I don't really know, but I have made some guesses, and I should like to share them with you.

Let's go back a while. A book I wrote twenty years ago – *The Floor of Heaven* (1992) – consisted of four long narrative poems, and was based partly on a story device employed in Luis Buñuel's funny and clever movie *The Discreet Charm of the Bourgeoisie* (1972), which features a sequence of dreams one within the other. It occurred to me many years ago that the meaning of a poem is like the meaning of a dream: intense, important, difficult to unravel and full of the energies of the unconscious mind.

And – though I have generally avoided the Juggernaut of Academia – I recently weakened (I needed the money) and completed a Doctor of Creative Arts degree at the University of Wollongong. Writing the doctoral thesis allowed me to explore this idea further. I won't drag you through all the details – the exegesis part of my thesis (where I reveal everything) is thirty thousand words long – but in brief, building on the work I did for my 1971 BA degree in Psychology, I followed Freud and Lacan through their various mirror-mazes and theories about dreams. Movies came next, and there the trail led from Slavoj Žižek to Alfred Hitchcock and back to Buñuel. In 1953, nearly twenty years before he made *The Discreet Charm of the Bourgeoisie*, he said:

Film is a magnificent and dangerous weapon if it is wielded by a free mind. It is the finest instrument we know for expressing the world of dreams, of feeling, of instinct. The mechanism that creates cinematographic images is, by its very function, the form of human expression most closely resembling the work of the mind during sleep. Film seems to be an involuntary imitation of dream ... the darkness that gradually invades the auditorium is the equivalent of closing our eyes. It is the moment when the nightly incursion into the unconscious begins on the screen and deep inside man.

I know no better way of exploring the movies I like – Alfred Hitchcock's *Vertigo*, for example, or Hitchcock's own favourite among his many movies, *Shadow of a Doubt* – than to read them as expensive, complicated, multi-authored, beautiful and sometimes terrifying dreams.

And what better way to interpret the oeuvre of Australia's most interesting poet, the non-existent Ern Malley? His every poem is a melange of incomprehensible images wrenched into an unwilling cohabitation, a process that liberated the vengeful unconscious fantasies of the collaborator hoaxers, the young poets James McAuley and Harold Stewart. The fecundity of those violent nightmares is still producing poems, plays, movies and paintings based on Ern Malley's invented life and writings, half a century or more after Ern's death, mainly by creative artists who weren't even born in his lifetime. In fact just as I was writing this Introduction a major new academic study of the Ern Malley affair landed on my desk.

To speak more calmly about the creative urge, Henry James's enigmatic story 'The Figure in the Carpet' (1896) comes to mind. In his well-known tale, James tells how a young critic seeks to unravel the secret theme or key that the famous (fictional) author Hugh Vereker says lies at the centre of everything he has written. It's visible, Vereker says, but hard to discern, like a subtle pattern woven into a carpet. Alas, after many plot twists and turns, no secret is found. The Bulgarian-French critic Tzvetan Todorov comes to an enlightened conclusion about this quest in his 1977 book *The Poetics of Prose* (translated by American poet Richard Howard):

If Henry James's secret, the figure in the carpet of his work, the string which unites the pearls of the separate tales, is precisely the existence of a secret, how does it come about that we can now name the secret, render absence present?

Am I not thereby betraying the fundamental Jamesian precept which consists in this affirmation of absence, this impossibility of designating truth by its name? But criticism too (including mine) has always obeyed the same law: it is the search for truth, not its revelation, a treasure hunt rather than the treasure itself, for the treasure can only be absent. Once this 'reading of James' is over, we must then begin reading James, set out upon a quest for the meaning of his oeuvre, though we know that this meaning is nothing other than the quest itself.

As John Ashbery suggested in 1995, there's not much point in trying to explain poems or to search for the meaning of a work of literature. But if it's true that poems are really dreams in disguise, neither is there any stable frame of reference from which to view and judge a parade of dreams. The dreamer is the last person to ask, which is why people who have baffling dreams often go to psychiatrists to ask the meaning of what they are going through. Sometimes the psychiatrist, with her or his independent viewpoint and long experience in such matters, hits the nail on the head; sometimes not. That's the role I seem to be stuck with, and as you can see I have been making the most of the opportunity without getting very far. Of course if you don't agree with my line of thinking, you can always ask for a second opinion.

Meanwhile, enjoy these fragments of dream-work, as Freud called it. And when you wake up tomorrow, if you're lucky, you'll have some dream-work of your own to think about.

John Tranter

The Sibyl's Avenue

The lovers strolled in a city
Park under the branches of smudged trees,
Ample sun leaked down the sky –
Autumnal oak-leaves fell
Scattering fragments of calligraphy.

All this, locked away, when a bell
Rings. Memory leaks, touching sunlight,
Though with a kind of ease
My hand draws back –
The sky isn't blue it's abstract.

Those who walk this modern
Avenue, do so to pay the rent in paradise.
No takers, no shared accom.
A man sells diluted methadone twice
From a garish mobile bar;

Burbling vapours from
His fuel, used cotton oil, curdle in the air;
Bent hot-dogs talk to strangers.
Still, the oak trees flower above us,
A canopy of lust – look over there,

The sparrows chitter just far
Enough away from a cat, who chitters back.
This, so you know who'll still be here,
As time repeats its fact.
When you come, bring Echo and Thanatos,

finally, you might raise a cheer.

Robert Adamson

Public Mourning

The history of tango has been cancelled
due to the sheikh's plunge. Mourn

for his apocryphal drowning
in a lake in Morocco. I'm joyous

at the prospect of this jacket
outliving my jumpers. Ecstatic

hookers amass savings, US$ 3,500
per job. I make nothing vaguely comparable

from whoring my mind. The history
of philosophy reduced to a memory

of a real conversation. Glider
accident. Rotund corpse floats. At least I'm warm.

Ali Alizadeh

Aubade

Did I once believe in the power of poetry?
Was I swaddled like a baby
in a blanket of words?

Did they whisper me awake
and lullaby me to my dreams?

Now I stand, awkward, vertical,
in static and glare.
I cannot hear the silence

or the words that linger beneath it,
echoes of some unremembered Arcady.

To those who have me by the throat
and would rather I didn't hear
even the simple rise

and fall of my own breath,
I say, 'You misunderstand

if you think that any poet
ever lived in a golden age.
Every one lived in this world

under house arrest. The only gold
they ever knew was the music

of their imaginations,
when, for a few brief
unfathomable moments,

they mistook the prison bars of their minds
for the harp strings of the heart.'

Richard James Allen

Function Centre

Resonant surgical anecdotes roll on:
spiral fractures from middle-aged skateboarding.
Old antipathies are instantly renewed:
'Still writing away for X-Ray Spex, I see!'
When it comes to stories of jumping the fence
– 'For years I had been walking insincerely' –
many think I told you so, some feel cheated.
Vanity comes creeping out through tiny cracks
to bask in the sun: It was so cold in there!
But what's-her-name still speaks just often enough
for her silence not to be significant.
Outside: fractured slabs of concrete glistening.
Frangipani flowers lie crushed in the round.

Departing steps have a pasty sibilance.
A pair of near-perfect strangers, one patting
pockets in search of a lighter, the other
returning to return a mistaken coat,
make the first moves of what could turn out to be
a long conversation begun at the end
of a reunion where late-bloomers gloated
over the popular blonde who peaked too soon.

Chris Andrews

An Apology

I am sorry I cannot publish your poem.
The subject of a lost ant is truly original
and the dialogue between said ant
and blade of grass is certainly moving
(it moved me to write you this note).
May I suggest the repetition of 'Mummy'
be rethought, as some reader is bound to
point out that ants do not have individual mothers,
nor are they able to weep. Of course,
poetic licence can allow such anomalies;
however, describing the ant as three
black peas with miniature Meccano legs
is rather a mixed metaphor, which fails
in the final stanza when the ant
becomes a shrunken horse.
And finally, the form of the poem,
although inventive, is quite difficult to read
as the words do not meet up around the antennae.

Jude Aquilina

Hugh Tolhurst, with Lines for a Poem

Scenery emerges from the picture like a train
just emerged Jolimont-way from the
tunnel system, Melbourne, 1966 – in time
for jewels and binoculars hung from the head
of a mule – all roads to Port Phillip Bay.
Young mother pegging diapers on a line –
a black crow in its pulpit yawning the day's
sermon to conscripts ganging the platforms –
flashing backyard suburban jingoisms.
We look back through the poem and see
only the wisteria creeping under the windows,
a trellis, a flyscreen door and dead lawn
a million miles from Saigon. The train rattles on
from station to station, parsing the signals,
numbing the arses of generations to come
without ever upsetting the status quo.
Arriving one day at the end of the road
like a detail conscientiously ignored until it
punches you in the eye – imagining some
real estate genius struggling to find metaphors
that fit the marketplace: southerly prospects,
ocean views, all modcons. Grey ships ply
the dun-coloured textbook waters and turn
into History. It's cold and you shiver a little.
Out beyond the big picture the refinery lights
are coming on – the tide heaves towards its
Bethlehem. A hundred years and nothing
remotely imaginable, thinking why here and
not some other place, far away under monsoon –
Agent Orange sunsets making hell a scenery.

But the poem is only a way to dream without
having to suffer – and it dreams us too,
on the other side where time is forever
advancing like a threat. Night stabs a thorn
into the mind's eye – we end where we began,
riding the line until the words stop. The
silent machines take us back out of the picture.
A train's windows flash past like cinema:
Something groans. Something else gets born.

Louis Armand

Portrait of Edith Murtone, fiction writer

Scarlet nail polish and lipstick.
Plastic surgery on her once-prominent nose.
Edith summers in Cornwall,
winters in Athens.

Her latest novel is selling well.
The cook, the gardener,
will receive a Christmas bonus,
compensation for enduring
Edith's moods and temper
when she finds living
harder than writing.

Characters like Clarissa and Harold
appear to her
as she drives,
as she walks along the river.

Clarissa,
eldest of two daughters,
an amateur botanist and watercolourist,
infatuated with her piano tutor.

Harold,
a neighbour's only son,
asthmatic, excused from sport.
Interested in astronomy
and the treasure underneath Clarissa's skirt.

Desire,
the primary emotion that moves plot and pen,
stirs the serpents in the garden,
coiled in the shade of the family tree.

Images crafted into words,
words crafted into images.
Truth and fiction,
lying down in the same bed,
entwined,
no longer strangers
to each other.

The white heat of writing –
thoughts, visions
becoming words,
lifting the writer and the reader
beyond the page,
to where the self is seen,
an ant
struggling with crumbs,
one day to be crushed
beneath a wind-blown twig.

On a good day, five thousand words.
On a bad day, the snapping in half of pencils –
the study mirror reflecting
Edith asleep on the sofa,
one shoe missing,
an empty brandy bottle
in her lap.

Edith waking
with hangover –
legs of straw on which
to inch and tilt
towards the horizon
of the kitchen sink,
a much-needed glass of water.

Edith
straightening cushions on the sofa,
lighting the day's first cigarette,
asking the walls
what post-war England could be
if Nigel's plane hadn't been
shot down over Berlin.

The roulette wheel spins,
the white ball
comes to rest on zero.

Not every player
will risk as much again.

Edith alone
with her characters.
Maybe in the next book,
Harold, through his telescope
will view the flare and fall of a comet,
an arc of light that once scarred the heavens,
now reduced to a photo, data in a journal.
Clarissa will disturb his ordered world
by becoming pregnant.

The characters' world changed by
a birth,
a wavering allegiance,
an affair revealed,
leaving a known path.

All that threatens and excites,
asks us to consider again
human nature
as it slithers away
from definition,
Edith will examine
in her next book.

Already she knows its title,
writes it out neatly
on a fresh sheet of paper.

Tomorrow will be a good writing day,
if tonight she's able
to sleep.

Peter Bakowski

The Funnies

The comics were best kept simple –
The Little King, Boofhead, Brenda Starr.
The King never spoke
& others spoke 'but briefly'
in his presence – announcing
something – this or that –
& the King would leap,
scowl or shrug,
exclamation mark
above his head.
I understood him
from an early age.
The cartoonist's
ineptitude
was essential: Boofhead's
Egyptian style
of ambulation,
his Egyptian surprise.
'The true archaic simplicity'
as someone might have said.
Arms akimbo, one leg lifted,
mouth open, his eyes – did I
ever see him sleep? – pools
of black.
The amateurish, confident
styling of Brenda Starr.
Where is that world now?
I wanna go there & roll
cigarettes, roll my own
smokes, as Dan Hicks
had it – later, in a more
sophisticated age –

an age that
looks back –
at the King affronted,
Boofhead flummoxed, or
Boofhead stymied,
Starr crying or
having a thought ...
looks back, looks back,
astonished at that innocence.

Ken Bolton

Volatile Condensate

My dream once for the north wing of the building –
a vast mural of Fred and Wilma, done
'after Poussin' – is on hold. Unregretted.

What do you say to Jackson Pollock in a lift?
Obviously, the numbers climb higher and higher,
and expensive graffiti gets pulled out of the wall

at midnight, and carried away on a truck. You say
Que sera, sera and duck. Straightening up, slowly,
I explain my other dream to him: Géricault's portrait

of the back of Delacroix's head in old age.
Jackson laughs – 'Like mine of Bill de Kooning
aged ninety!' he says. Downstairs we throw the spray cans on
the fire – watch them explode.

Ken Bolton & John Jenkins

Others in the Town

for Newstead, Victoria: 3462

She is walking on frost at dawn
beside the highway that runs through the town
Over the bridge with a full river below
With black gloves on, she is planning for the town
Picking up a flattened beer can
Putting it in her pocket

then thinking of the four boyfriends she had
before she met Bill and settled down
Tucker · Ross   Bonici   Smith
and then Bill Menangartowe
who gave her the horsewhip
that he plaited with the three king browns
the ones he killed especially
        how many men have killed things ... especially, she thought

the whip hangs on the wall of the long-drop
with the view of the mountain
where ghosts maintain fame
        through legendary gambling debts
          bestiality
          leaning on the shovel at
          shallow graves of native men

Bill Menangartowe is home
dreaming of new teeth
so he can eat Harcourt apples and his wife's dry roast beef
that he complains of
       there he is
waking
pushing himself from noisy bed springs
    recognising his father's thumbs
as he pushes shells into the gun
crows and lambs sewn together in the distance
    are the crows complaining?
    have the lambs had their eyes pecked out?

Bill walks barefoot across the floor and out the door
Into work boots striped by slivers of dawn

He hunts for rabbits
the old-time meal
a recipe that only the older women know
from years ago
when mothers were few around here
    wondering
over cups of tea punctuated by sounds of a sparrow hunt
    how tiger snakes got into linen cupboards
and how people were allowed to swim nude in the Loddon river
    when the town has a policeman

When the moon is up her house is quiet

she can't sleep though
there is too much to plan

for the others in the town
on their fourth new start at a life
And those still on their first, awake,
from the night before
gambling online
through cups of tea
that are made
when the internet connection drops out

     She imagines the town as blue feathers
and all the children safe under wings

But a south-easterly pushes cloud into the moon
and her pillow goes dark
the wind pushes the colossal gum tree that saw the start of fences
     saw white rapes
black births

                      heard the secret songs
   and all the fights that followed
its trunk, full of wire, beer bottles, and horseshoes
an unknown baby skeleton

the wind pushes at the tree
and it falls in the dark
without a sound

Neil Boyack

Clarity of the word

to cut; to run; to stay in a burrow underground; to impersonate a tree in autumn; to approach the world with an open heart and an infinite capacity for disappointment; *nm* rapturous dismay; joyful ingratitude; *nf* a type of boxing match used for divination or to contact the dead; a woman who lives off the immoral earnings of more than three husbands; (*S Am*) a pitchfork with an angel's heart; as in (*Cu*) the termites have crawled into the piano, or (*DR*) he who drinks the sea must nurse the oyster; (*RPL, Chi*) unworthy of entering a shopping mall even in a cyclone; (*Per, Ec*) gifted with fingers small enough to befriend dustmites; (*Mex, Col, Ven*) not to be trusted, not to be believed, also patron saint of fish; (as a colour) yellow, orange, red or brown; (*ornith.*) a seabird with golden wings and hard onyx beak or a small bird afraid of swamps seen only during ill-omened festivities; from Arabic, a tree that befriends doomed travellers; also see medieval Latin, a table for unwritten books; (*colloq.*) to succeed, to fail, to cough, to lose one's way etc.

Peter Boyle

The Sublime

at eighty-six and ninety-one they are still together
more or less
and greet me at the door
as if I am the punchline to a joke
they were just recalling

my mother staggers sideways in the drive
my father reaches for a wall, a rail, an arm
with the urgency telephones demand

they know what it is now
and do their best to hide this knowledge from us
agreeing to be forgetful and ever more frail
they can't help grinning at the picture they must make

they expect to be driven to appointments
they say are medical or therapeutic

my mother toys with the idea of a new knee
my father trembles to the tiny drum machine
beneath his ribs

and their eyes go cloudy, ears a solid silent blue,
their mouths half open to let out the unspoken
because they know what it is
and now they want it more than this old world

the small days come, flowers in the garden,
drugs delivered to the door, postcards in the box outside

she has a sturdy stick to hold down against this earth
tapping as if to wake someone down there

a warning they are coming

Kevin Brophy

In my phone

for Gig

you said we didn't but we did
    have telephones
        in seventies share houses,
bulky bakelite telephones
    ringing as often
        as Frank O'Hara's
and Brigid Berlin's did, a decade earlier

we had honour systems –
        add phone calls
           to a running total
    in a column under your name,
like a boardgame score,
              pay up
when the household bill arrives

*

I could ring to say
        sometimes I imagine you
    in a Max Ernst collage
        (*Une semaine de bonté*)

there's a woman reflected
        in an ornately gilded mirror
                behind an open door,
you're the other woman
        guiding a feathered bird-man
        into a high Edwardian
                drawing room –
he carries a tooled leather bag,
        he seems to be a doctor,
'mind how you go doctor' you say
        'just step over
            the apopleptic monkey, doctor'

doctor feathered bird-man
            brings sleeping elixir,
        an anodyne

*

in sleep
        I'm filled with thought,
    my dream constructed
            not by surrealism
                but by Slabs R Us,
    solid, solemn, grey

half asleep, half dreaming,
        a phone is ringing,
            I hold the earpiece close –
    friends pollute the swoony hours
            with caring

in a poetry world
     everything is providential,
               or not,
and, sometimes,
          just life on hold, call waiting,
     like Tennyson's poetic

reading now, quiet,
               a newer title –
     I always skip
               redacted poems,
the crossings-out seem obvious
     and attention seeking –
you would agree?
          your number's in my phone,
     I could call to ask.

Pam Brown

tick

last drinks at the
friendship bar evanescence
is my pashmina no apology
for the lack of a biography
anyone could see it
coming runes in the fettuccini
is one way of looking at it i
suppose all the decades of
romping in the hay production
figures never disputed now it's
time to leave the wagon to
serenade its own wheels   how
black the glossy stars this enchanted
evening mario stranger than anything you
could call terrestrial bow ties

Joanne Burns

How the Dusk Portions Time

Then one evening, after the gallery, hung with invisible
abstracts, you take me apart to flesh the miniatures:
a fleck of craquelure, speckles of mascara from my
      shadow eyes, already panda-streaked.

I fail to notice how you slip the pieces in your coat pocket.
Distracted as I am by wolf hands, the hairs in your cleft
neck. You're not, but you might be, up yourself, I think,
      skating across the vestibule floor.

How the light divides the dream, menacing, promising
shyness or indifference, I cannot tell, though it amounts
to the same verdict. Is that what you mean about pleading
      guilty as the fig trees stir, balmy in winter?

Some evenings are this fragile. Rainbow lorikeets court
the soft crumbs, a magpie takes off with a crust, clouds
skim over the Finger Wharf, footsteps trip in the Domain
      where the pine scent lingers as lips:

ours for a flower moment, the botanist's pinnate rose
is a name calling to its mute echo. Bats skip and loop
the legible sky in their quiet frenzy like involuntary
      kites between metallic and neon spires.

So dusk emulsifies desire, or maybe it's the reverse
– we are tenants of this periphrastic end. Office cubicles
half-lit, ladder the sky, turning their discretionary gaze
      to what's sketched by the carbon ink.

Michelle Cahill

the lights are on

the irony of green rain
is not lost on you

the rank apocalypse
stalks the landscape

spreadable butter for your convenience
where would we be without

your depressive head
mocks you from its alcove

cars whizz both ways
the question remains

like a daytime tv show
where someone you're sure

is yourself in disguise
makes predictable jokes

laughed at by machines

Grant Caldwell

on empty

On a hot day the North-West Plain is so flat it isn't.
The horizon curves and stirs like a wisp of moustache.
Animals burrow that aren't meant to burrow.
Prey walk past their predators under a white flag.
The eyes of roadkill are left to boil in their sockets.
The can of beer is dry when you open it.
A cigarette is rolling another swagman.
The motor smokes nervously before you start it.
The mobile phone sweats, whimpers and croaks.
The devil is on holiday in Tasmania.
The paddock on the left is Texas.
The seat of government is the only tree.
We'll take a rest-stop at the next mirage.
Is it far? It has been. Are we there yet? No.

John Carey

Magma

      At almost noon.

He sees only figures   no game.

    They clap. Céline has the ball.
       He raises his palms, then lowers them.

Just go, just go. Clap, laugh, go.

      Their shadows curl
under them: falling leaves.
The ball hovers above the beach, eclipsing the sun a few inches.
He eases back
he becomes sand.

Bonny Cassidy

ms marbig No. 26 16

another team needs restructuring
her boss seeks rejuvenation
he likes a shiny new worker

in glossy black accessorised with chrome
she's the facilitator who holds the coalface together.
strong jaw   teeth without stains
she click-clacks his documents

past your use-by date, he
exposes her in public
whips her back into an angry V.
her rusty assistants jam
printers, shredders, fax machines

Julie Chevalier

We begin building that which cannot collapse because it will have to have been built as if it had already fallen

Gary was being extremely annoying with the glue-gun, as a
     parody
buffoon gets stuck to the routine and then can only separate
by ripping off his own souls while his kaleidoscopic pantaloons
spiral outta control like a flotilla of combi-vans
driven by acid-hippies through the violet hill-deserts of ma
     mind...
do you too smell the blood of a nationalised energy foundation?
You have to keep the abecedaria flying, or, if not flying, at least
     floppily erect!
(uh-oh, here comes that dynamic psychotherapy again, Gwyneth,
you're for it now! It'll make you springen, springen wiff 'appenis
     fer sure,
as the flashers go off with epilepsy-inducing arrhythmia.)
Please don't bother me with your body any longer, I've enough
of orgasms and orgies to last me ten thousand lifetimes,
and it's a better bet to go pale over a flaccid biopic of a pallid
     poet,
because my wound-dark nerve-endings are just sooooo sensitive
     they quiver
at the merest trilling of those much speculated-upon boronic
     microparticles –
Fargh! your vulgar disinhibiting fanfare can be only dreadful
     noise to me!

Justin Clemens

Picasso

Wrapped in bulls and balls,
squiggle me macho.
Seek out my women,
how I make their
bums, breasts and bellies
fold up into furniture,
gore them into dripping tears.
I am potted, baked dry,
moulded by España's rough hands.
If you are woman don't catch the
attention of my one red eye.

Sue Clennell

Four Lines by Ezra Pound

The New Zealand poet settled to his coffee at the Astoria in
  Lambton Quay
kindly hunched against the bitter wind at an outside table
  because although
he hated us when smokers ruled the world he pities us these
  days of leprosy.

He spoke of our late mutual friend from Lecce who, whilst
  living in Venice,
paid his respects to Ezra Pound on occasion – as one would –
  the poet sunk
below the waterline into the clarity of incommunicado and
  monkish accidie.

One day the poet raised his head and spoke – four lines –
  from out the deep
of his mistake – four good strong tough lines that anyone
  could remember
and the man from Lecce did and they became the punchline
  for a story.

But but – I said. *I have read those lines, unattributed, in a book
  of verse.*
Four good, strong, tough lines that were worth remembering,
  and so I did.
Such Antipodean chutzpah to plagiarise Pound, his brilliant
  rottenness.

Jennifer Compton

Metamorphosis

The mother is now the child
and the daughter scolds her
for driving late at night
and the mother cowers
on the sofa half afraid of her.

Her disgruntled child seems
taller and stronger than she remembers
and the daughter goes into the kitchen
to cook some beetroot broth
and then they sit in the lounge room

quietly together, not a word spoken
and then the mother nods off
to sleep watching television
and the daughter carries her
to the bed and watches her mother

dream and she stands over
guarding the bed like some Roman sentry
and then finally she goes to bed to plan
the next day and this is love
in a strange disguise, but love nonetheless.

Michael Crane

Adenocarcinoma Triolet

They've found something nasty
    In the small bowel.
They need to be hasty,
They've found something nasty
And not very tasty.
    Throw in the towel!
They've found something nasty
    In my small bowel.

Fred Curtis

Metropolitan Cannibal Hymn

Master of Stomachs, our powers have greyed
absorbed for congruent, apparent eternity.
Hustle and bustle, gristle and grit are no match
for something you cannot pass first.

Lord of Starlessness, lumbering slob!
Skyscraper, babel of crockery, serves you.
Windlicked streets trawl for dross.

Night Sky Swallower, infinite oesophagus,
holes in your mouths become mouths in our holes.
How has the meal of our brains not killed you?
Same goes, O Indigestible Gape.

Toby Davidson

Mini-series

mais qui voit la fleur, dont voir le soleil

Dawn, clock-face of the heavens, becomes
momentous with fulfilment, birds
with the eccentricity of minutes, wake,
launch themselves into the unfolding
air of time, each with its own beady
reading of history: insects too
stir into action and that same air
in its bland magnanimity, takes them in
as the Cash Converters down below
open their everlasting doors to the latest
needy – the world at large is ready for
business: early ants carting home
the injured and the accidentally dead,
young magpies squawking for
another handout and the heart
punching the body's bundy only yet
half-awake to what may come
down the chute to it before
the next night signs it off …

Bruce Dawe

Afterimage

The image lit against the eye's dark lid
is often clearer than the light of day.
Sometimes I see the view amended:

the missing key, the winter tree inverted
as a photo negative, a blazing x-ray
of the image lit against the eye's dark lid.

In conversation, details that were hid
may come to light in such or such a way
(for better or for worse)   the view's amended.

It shows what's dimmed and what's illuminated,
the shifting chiaroscuro. Who's to say
the image lit against the eye's dark lid

is closer/further from the one intended?
And what directs the cutting room, the replay
– where sometimes the truth can be amended?

With luck, by second chance I'm visited
by definition in a field of grey;
in the image lit against the eye's dark lid,
I sometimes see the view amended.

Sarah Day

Homage to Mapplethorpe

When a perfect purple iris
pokes out its lovely tongue
at the tulip's scarlet lips;
and the pose of a half-open rose
near a deep-throated daffodil
provokes a pansy's frown,
but the daisy winks a dark eye;
then the watching calla lily
exposes an urgent stamen.
Passing bees all raise their eyes
though none of it comes as a huge surprise.

Suzanne Edgar

'You know the way ...'

You know the way a snatch of song lodges in your brain and
    won't be shifted no matter how you try to trick it out the
    door?

Well, this morning 'Amazing Grace' has come to stay, just the
    tune and those two words; the bits about 'no sweeter sound'
    and 'save a wretch like me'

disregarded somewhere else. Which is not so strange as I
    don't believe in 'lost' and 'saved' but I do know forms
    of grace exist

and are amazing. I think of a dancer's grace as she glides into
    the air, or the diver's equal grace gliding towards the sea:
    the body in defiance of its limitations,

going through, beyond. Graceful, gracious, gracile, words that
    multiply and spread like flowering vine. Grace notes of
    unbelief that still restore the faith.

I'd like to be standing by the laundry door looking at snow
    piled high in the backyard and stretching away to distant
    hills, all deep silence and soft light,

indistinctions that are pliable and hint at more and more
    concealment. Here, today, each leaf and branch is clear,
    and even shadows are

unsentimentally direct. Surface is baked surface and heat
    haze won't bear comparison with mist, won't let me think
    transcendence.

The following is true. The water in the bay is pristine, amazing
  shades of green, a random morse of light, the sea flushing
  between rocks with the gentle pop and splash

that avoids monotony. But in the channel, among the leaves
  and weed and scraps of paper, two dead seabirds – black
  and bloated – bob in the push and pull,

their wings flared and fixed in mimicry of flight, their feet
  flexed as though they were about to land.

And now I'm stuck in the feedback loop: adrift in sun, snow,
  amazing grace, dead birds. The binary brain looking for
  a way out or in between,

a way to celebrate without appearing selfish or simple-minded,
  without me at the centre pulling strings or getting out the
  bubble wrap,

without an image of the imageless, or an image of the world
  devoid of people to make the whole thing work, the dream,

uncalled for, undeserved, of the present expanding as if there
  is no future or the future is this presence, that leafless tree
  against the sky,

the glittering humpbacked sea, the thousand flickering things
  the mind lights on and tries to hold.

Brook Emery

Chrome Arrow

Cento for Pam Brown

If I could take a flight from zero
to infinity, get lost nearby
that *Eloquence* – now I am free!
Atomic rocks
form like hills & dunes,
like grass. I do a lot of thinking.
Sky goes rococo as the nearest dream
is led away. We behave badly
in dangerous clothes & laugh for days.
I want to remember this chaos,
song of one breath in A.
Phantoms on the home stretch
call my name. Bird magician
sugar   concrete
a woman opening the heavy door.
There are no lyrics left
& another reality howls
as the new gets
newer. I stood exactly where
those piles of books carried me.
Over ruins of this comedy
I lie surrounded by beauty
until the Pleaides blink
like a sparkler in the HaHa Room.

Kate Fagan

Terns

who fly epic arcs, slipping through
atmospheres, past sleeping continents –
so good at bathing, too: cajoling brine
over wings with shivering leaps backwards
then a final shimmy ten feet above
as if to baptise their former selves.
Next, the charisma of flight – their bodies
such an ingenious fit with the world
as they side-swipe the wind, ride its back
to reconnoitre the river, make lightning-culls
from the hearts of sudden white flowers.
Later they stand, dumpy yet winsome
on mirror sand, facing out to sea:
their eyes calm, gleaming like homely stars.

Diane Fahey

Mother's (creative) tempat

She surrounded the wounded but courageous
love of her life with objects, and more objects
than you can imagine but which sometimes he
wanted to leave behind, and he'd pace the house
like a placid, intelligent but caged animal taking
this as his reality: the pictures on the wall, the
patterns on the carpet, the many figurines and
gaily patterned porcelain, joyously acquired
on outings together to exhibitions and galleries,
she also asked him to search for and research
whenever he felt any sickness coming on again,
relatives were persuaded to leave them objects
and paintings in their wills, adding even more
complexity to this, their private gallery, which I'd
dream about in terms of a gift shop and then
wonder when, finally, we would open the doors
to the public? but my mother kept on collecting,
she even studied Art to become a volunteer gallery
guide, never a word passing her lips about why,
and when I dared to say, near the end of her life,
that I often wondered whether there was anything
'wrong' with Father, she turned and looked at me
in silence, with the sworn secrecy of the Resistance
Father took, along with ECT Amnesia, to his grave.

Jeltje Fanoy

Motherlogue

Whenever I start a narrative poem she says *God*
God God, so you can take that for granted: I'm
editing her responses. This is the yarn of, well,
you'll recognise it (and imagine her with her hands
over her ears as she does the washing up: with
her elbows I suppose). After my third there was
a swan and then a suckling pig. I'd find myself
hanging out clothes in my underwear – or my husband's –
and the neighbours drawing the blinds at each other,
saying, she's not really adjusting to Wahroonga
is she? They – inside my own house – have eaten
me a hole in the couch, and I'm doing the accounts
with one hand and killing a snake with another
while I get an armful of wood. But after a few wines
and a few accidental discounts 'at' work, (I have
an online business) I'm ready for Joint Family
Suicide: one of our 'TV games'. *God God God*
adding rhythm. Then my eldest comes in with blood
on his face from fighting with some Pymble trash
and says we're out of water. So I gather up the
tribe: one or two boys, one or two girls, the swan
and the suckling pig, and we head towards the
Lindfield reservoir, each of us with the biggest
water vessel we can carry. Then there's a shift
in critique, she's saying *you can't*, meaning I can't,
tell a woman's story. But I am telling it. Mariah
(named after the wind, not the singer), has crawled
into a crocodile, and I didn't even know they had
crocodiles on the North Shore, but I'm only a girl
from Nimmitabel with a horde of kids of one kind
or another walking the edge of the road, wine bottles
in hand playing sweet, sweet music with their little

breaths. The swan gets in after her, and I wouldn't
want to be a crocodile on the other end of a swan.
I think the swan left a torn Coke can in the croc
for good measure. And Mariah comes out all slimy
and beaming with some sorry overbred excuse
for a Wahroonga hound, saying, Mummy, look
I found a puppy! And I say, hooray, what are you
going to feed it on? But there's a crow eating a
possum as we turn the corner, and Mariah's got
her waddy so she shoos the crow on the head and
puts it in her dilly bag and sets the little socialite
with its faux diamond collar's kisser in the pre-
pecked possum. *Uh, animal cruelty? Examples*
to children? I hear over the lino vacuuming. Bush
rules, I say. It's starting to get dark, and as I'm
new to this builtup area (only having recently moved
here from Belconnen) it seems very strange and
eerie. The houses here truly have no season, no
blossom, and the lawns have no smell. I had a couple
of cones earlier and a slight feeling of paranoia
begins to resurface. But as anyone who thought
of it would say, you can't drink paranoia (let alone
have a bubble bath in it or boil spuds). So we head
on, but I'm glad I brought my shotgun. The kids
and co. are all wearing their scapulas, too. So when
the Devil rides up on a horse, I'm terrified but stand
my ground. Nice little herd of pigs you got, he
says, stroking the dead lamb in his lap. He broke
into my consciousness with that one I said to Trent
later. I'll give you a waterbag for the boy, he said,
not pointing at my oldest, but at Jess, my androgynous
third, and I said no deal. Give us a billy out of
the good of your heart, I said. And while I waited
on his reply I chanted Hail Mary, full of grace,
the Lord is with thee, and he said, Nema eartson

sitrom aroh ni te cnun. Which sounded like nothing
but I soon realised was the Ave Maria in backwards
Latin. And I said, in forwards Spanish, Dios te
salve, María, llena eres de gracia. And the Devil
replied Nema etrom artson alled aro'llen osseda
(in backwards Italian), so I said, grabbing the billy
by the handle as I did so, and mentally thanking
the Portuguese nun I'd studied with, Avé Maria,
cheia de graça, o Senhor é convosco. And he grabbed
the handle too with his bony hand like Voss come
out of the desert to steal my children, my honeybees,
muttering in his best better backwards French accent,
Nema trom erton ed erueh'l à te tnanetniam. I shot
half his head off then, yelling fit to rouse the Nazis
from their Master Chefs in Hell, Gegrüßet seist
du, Maria, voll der Gnade, der Herr ist mit dir!
I knew I was out of languages, and I could tell he
was ready with backwards Tagalog. Jess gave me
her/his saw and I cut off the Devil's fingers
and took the billy: it was a diabolical billy and
never emptied. So we threw our bottles into the
bushes and headed home, thinking that Trent would
probably be home from the bank by now. Steeds
of Satan though are faster than lightning, and we
got home an hour earlier than we'd left. So I decided
not to smoke the second time round. Gave Mariah
a pot to cook the crow in, and did some journalling.
It looked like we could make ourselves at home
in Wahroonga after all. I can hear exaggerated
yawning from the bedroom, so I'll leave the story
there, put the garbage out and the kettle on, and
go in to the love of my life. My witchetty's at half-
mast already. Bon voyage-nuit!

Michael Farrell

Warning

In the bay-window's corner,
a cobweb has come unstitched;
time dangles, is unturned at the
beginning of a cosmic fall;

after six months of mail we are
to meet. Face-to-face existence
promises miraculous guilt
for the experience. Proof
that what is natural is trouble.

Johanna Featherstone

Gli ultimi zombi

for Ezra

What it must be to be buried on an island
                    of the dead like a character
in some Uwe Boll zombie rave up.

The back alleys stuffed to the ceiling
                    with overpriced pepperoni pizzas
and the stench of fish soaking damp laundry.

On the Grand Canal the vaporetto lists
                    a city park drunk stumbling
at every oversubscribed port of call.

Like cattle at the famous Roma sales
                    the befuddled subjects adoringly
compliant servants to the tyranny of the viewfinder.

Liam Ferney

Fluff

Milling about the city's nightlife,
she threads through the quilted crowd
who rug themselves up, flattering
each other's leathers and wispy flair.
She stands on the fringe like a lost
strand of hair, listening to the needles,
the knit-knot words, the pinning-up of
phrases – cottoning on to their lingo.
She's ready to be brushed aside
when some guy's quip poufs her up
like a pillow, though she responds by
chewing a ball of fluff because, for
some fuzzy reason, she wants his hide,
sewing what's left of her heart to
her sleeve – a threadbare cliché that
his quiff-like puns pierce like
a pin-cushion. With conversation
wearing thin, his hand reaching for
her velvet, she remembers the lint
piling up in the corners of her
apartment; the frayed curtains she's
never closed on her view of the city.
She can see it now from her bedroom
window: the silhouetted skyline, a
tattered hem; the stars, little white
cross-stitches forming a sky of blind
eyes; and rolling over the buildings,
the moon, a silver ball of wool,
unravelling.

Toby Fitch

Long Weekend, 2

The elephant is the comparative immaculateness
of the empty rooms at my parents' holiday house.
Arriving at any such place in breezy, bayside night
will present an identical scene; dull, dormant light
flickering alive the photo frames, fanned-out old magazines,
specially made beds with directions to extra linen,
remote controls with channel guides handwritten
in tentatively proud script, a fridge filled by bare essentials
& the fresh stuff you know yr mum snuck in the day before.
There is a poignancy in such presentation I can barely endure.
Ostensibly I just chuckle or say the minuteness makes me grin.
Within, what recurs inexplicably is the thing Thomas Jefferson
said about the art of life being the avoidance of pain. I know
my mum got catharsis from cleaning every corner of my
    grandfather's
joint when he passed away. I don't presage a speck
worth shifting when my parents move on. What will be left
down here except a stasis of lovingly arranged invitation?
Sometimes I envisage it being best if I were to never shed light
on such cordiality again, but just to let it decay behind
thick blinds matted with dust only airborne to opportunistic
burglars on the most sun-filled & silent weekdays.

William Fox

The Suns Fall at Zero

The zebra measured shimmering lines to a yellow slippery dip,
    pacing service station skeleton awning –
I considered a sideboard where it lay in the street,
counted five long dashes as a girl reflected cool against gushed
    drainage,
pink fibre folds hid under happy green wrapping lying about
    her closed eyes.
Someone had abandoned a white, black-wheeled tractor; its
    blue bucket matched her bikini top.
'Should we really be where these tents are in our blue and
    white swimwear?'
I read and ignored a drip from boned eave.
She lay out on the tarmac, a bikini sphinx, her swimmers eaten
    by movement over
the waiting slippery dip, against a purple galaxy, with the
    shadow of Ned Kelly's horse hiding out.
At her waist things had gone awry,
it was at this point you could note, if not distracted by riveted
    cement rampart,
blackened buildings which stood dilapidated; ink splatter
    encroaching to slick surfaces.
She lay, legs an easy knee calf-high cross – out, owning the
    rigid grip of gutter
below she mirrored still,
under fallen arm white dashed tar trembled the plastic curl of
    the slippery dip,
flames boiled from where the people had been,
I saw charcoal smear constellations; one green pylon blurred
    aqua where it met the rip,
written armed line, hip under string, cappuccino skin,
bellicose consumption, between bitumen and shoulder and
    neck, a small echo of the coming storm.

Her swimsuit cup matched the tractor's bucket: it was an
   unusual coincidence.
'Should we really be where these tents are in our blue and white
   swimwear?'
The words slowly dissolved as stars jammed from the other side
   of the wall,
only where the cleaner worked had anything come through.
The far right corner saw the slim frames of the city bombed out
   of the wilderness.
Plants still lived in the drain,
heavy lines of crossing fled from her hand into froth where she
   threw up the familiar pool.
Forefront steel points loomed away gold flares sank,
I wondered why someone left the dining room cabinet in the
   middle of it all, let it be graffitied,
and I realised that the building was just bones, I could see the
   storm.
A few more suns fell 'Why was she the only one running?' A few
   rusty bloody, hung on.

Andrew Galan

The Sum and its Parts

Not a rerun of *Star Trek:*
The Next Generation or a reload of *I*
Love Lucy but the day in my head replayed
and the nervous system closed up

– when I got to the burial ground
summer had already come looking in
to the light-filled hole
the child on his rocking horse, distinct
in his world, horn and ears alert.

Did I say this was a love story?
The pressure of new sap faced with love
embodied: vapour-clouded, breathless.

When Actaeon went into the forest
it was full summer, all that tells of the season
said differently through sunshine.

So late in the year. We step through this
curtain, to crouch, where last night's windfall
lies bruised upon the grass

the upturned forest in sad decline, the pity of it,
so meekly arriving, dog-helmeted as you
and I console ourselves.

The problem is not flesh and bone but viscera,
the shining consciousness it maintains
as beauty, hard above the poisoned blood.

Angela Gardner

Absurdity Rules

sometimes   being cheerful isn't easy
that ability to smile at someone else's child
throwing a public tantrum & having the discipline
not to abuse the bus driver   when he's
forty minutes late   & trying not to flinch
when someone says of a recently deceased relative
– I wonder what wonderful adventures she's having –
no   your default position is a *sweet dour pessimism*
where the soundtrack of your days   is a Brahms
string sextet   but you can bring out the hilarity
in bleakness   like the Hanged Man   turn everything
on its head   so even the worst calamity can be
laughed at

> *my way of laughing*
> *is to tell the truth*

so the only real catastrophe occurs   when your pen
runs out   while trying to record a *Chaser* Moment
& those belle epoque Rupert Bunny women   clutching
fans & roses & staring existentially into the night
could they be waiting for a take-away pizza?   then
while the lights are off   an auteur projects a
fictional film of your life-in-progress   but
the plot is vertiginous   the colour palette
confusing (even rainbows have doppelgangers)   the
protagonist is unlikeable & it's no joke   when
she misplaces her sanity   then discovers her soulmate
is a pedophile serial killer

> *comedy is a tragedy*
> *with a happy ending*

Carolyn Gerrish

Leftovers from a pirate party

OFFER: very small
dog coat Lewisham
4 used netballs
Old goth/punk clothes,
size 12–14
WANTED: Heat mat
(for hermit crab aquarium)
Inflatable Santa – giveaway or loan
OFFER: Three-arm chandelier
with frosted glass –
needs rewiring
LEFTOVERS FROM
A PIRATE PARTY
Jade plant from Mascot
gone already!
RE-OFFER: Disposable diapers
for small cat/dog
3 vacuum cleaners,
no wands
WANTED: 7 fence palings
LARGE CONTAINERS
FOR HOME BREW
To the Lady who I gave
Sony Trinitron TV to in Feb!
OFFER: Yabby family
of five in Glebe
Mixed Things From
My Pantry: Riverwood
Two shopping bags
full of stuffed bears etc

Jane Gibian

An Uncertain Future

I was sitting in my car opposite
the Adelaide Magistrates Court
    waiting on a change of lights
when i first saw her

she was in her early twenties
    had on a black sleeveless top
& a denim mini skirt
    her arms & legs were heavily
tanned & she wore strappy sandals

her hair was bottle blonde –
    & as she crossed in front of me
blowing out a stream of blue
cigarette smoke
    i noticed her black roots
complimented her chipped & broken
front teeth

she was at least seven months pregnant

the lights changed
    i moved off slowly –
into my own uncertain future.

Geoff Goodfellow

Dreams and Artefacts

after the Titanic Artefact Exhibition

I.
Patiently, ticket by ticket, a soft-stepped crowd
advances into the mimic ship's hull half-
sailed out of the foyer wall, as if advancing into
somebody else's dream –
the interior, windowless, where perspex cases bear,
each to its single light, small relics –
a tortoiseshell comb, an ivory hand-mirror,
a necklace pricked with pin-sized costume pearls.
They might be mine – at least, things loosed
from a dream I had, off and on, for years.
They have suffered nothing, these things raised
from a place less like place than like memory itself –

II.
Where the sea is
worked back upon itself in soundless storm,
          a staircase climbs.
Its scroll of iron foliage grows in subtler garlands now –
it is the sea's small
machinery of hunger, feeding on iron, makes these
          crookedly intricate festoons,
as if it were the future of remorse – Piece by piece,
the staircase returns
                    to the conditions of dream.

III.
In the next room, they have custom-built a staircase.
A replica, reinvented from a photograph,
it leads nowhere – or it leads to the house of images
where nothing is lost. A clock without a mechanism
adorns its first-floor landing, hands stopped at that minute
history pours through. We forgive things
only because we own them – This is a staircase
not for climbing, its first step strung with a soft-weave rope.

IV.
It is raining as I leave –
long rain breaking itself onto the footpath,
breaking easily into the surface of itself
like a dream without emblems, an in-drawn shine.
Overhead, clouds build and ruin imaginary cities,
slow-mo historical epics with the sound down,
                              playing to no one.

Lisa Gorton

Flying Foxes

In the night, the gorging begins
again, in the spring
night, in the branches
of the Moreton Bay figs,
that are fully-rigged
as windjammers, and make a flotilla
along the street.
And from the yard-arms
are strung clusters
of hanged sailors,
canvas-wrapped and tarred –
these are the bats, come
for the split fruit, and dangled,
overturned where they land.
It is the tobacco fibrils
in the fruit they seek,
and those berries, when gouged,
are spilt, through the squall
of the crowd, like
a patter of faeces
about the bitumen. This amidst
the cloudy shine
of the saline
streetlamps. In the ripe nights
the bats fumble and waste
what they wrest –
there's a damp paste
upon the road,
which dries to matted
sawdust, soon after the day's

steam has reared; it is scraped
up by the shovel-load.
The bats are uncorked
like musty vapour, at dusk,
or there is loosed a fractured
skein of smoke, across
the embossed lights
of the city. The moon is lost,
to an underhanded
flicked long brush-load of paint.
You think of the uncouth ride
of the Khan and his horde,
their dragon-backed shape
grinding the moon
beneath its feet.
And then, of an American
anthem, the helicopters
that arrive with their *whomp whomp*
whomp. I'm woken
by the bats still carrying on
in the early hours,
by the outraged screech,
the chittering
and thrashing about
where they clamber heavily,
as beetles do, on each other's backs.
They are Leonardo
contraptions. They extend
a prosthetic limb,
snarl, and knuckle-walk
like simians, step
each other under
and chest-beat, although

hampered with a cape. In sleep
I trample the bedsheet
off, and call out
'Take that!' (I am told),
punching the pillow in the heat.
I see the fanged shriek,
and the drip
of their syringes,
those faces with the scowl
of a walnut kernel.
It's some other type of bat
I think of: these, in books,
where I looked them up,
have a face you can imagine
if you recall how you'd whittle
finely at a pencil
and moisten the lead
with the tongue-tip –
a little face that belies its greed,
like that of an infant.
All partly autonomous things
trample others down,
even what is their own,
and the whole earth throbs
and smoulders
with pain. No comfort for us that
in the nights I have seen
how the living pass
about the earth,
that is deep with the ashes
of the dead, and quickly, too,
vanish into dark,
like will o' the wisps

thrown out of the sun.
At three o'clock I gather
our existence
has been a mistake. I would like
to turn my back on
its endless strife;
but when I look out
at the night, I am offered
otherwise only
the chalk-white, chaste
and lacklustre moon.

Robert Gray

-kuing the Rex

The mathematician rises
to explore parabolic form
the Rex cat sleeps

Purl wave ever
the stylish beehive
bum in my face

Bred into delicate
frame... running true
the Cornish wrecker

In Hearty Street
where two or three
may gather

Merly the Rex
is assuredly in
the midst of them

Kathryn Hamann

Busker and Chihuahua, Chapel Street

He plays an old cicada-shell guitar
his belongings dishevelling a faded blue blanket.

A tape-deck, a pink ice-cream bucket, a tattered glove
(falconer's or biker's?), its leather scarred by talons (gravel?),

and his white Chihuahua elegantly avoiding all eyes –
disdainful as a mannequin to out-mannequin god.

Shopfronts were passing like a glance, a glassy shrug
and I noticed the slithery rail in Brave where dresses hung

like marked-down lungs. I photographed the dog's silvery fur
his hand-knitted jacket of dark arguing wool

snug around torso and haunches – drop-stitched, ragged –
it was a cold winter day to be busking outdoors

near the florist, near the pet shop, near Coles.
Each time the busker played Clapton's 'Layla',

the dog's ears twitched with minuscule approval.
Kaiser rolls were steaming in the Daily Bell bakery

but like Pierrot's chiens savants, the Chihuahua was guarding
his master's alms: a demi-baguette, a pink ice-cream bucket

of coins; and the glove tossed on a pale blue blanket
like a hand begging all alone on the sea.

Jennifer Harrison

Through a Window, Looking Back

At last, she thought, looking back
through the train's jiggling window,
seeing the Italian countryside
like a Giorgione landscape.
But what was this 'at last' –
it was hardly being here
away from family and domestic routine,
though, it's true, she'd longed for that;
for an absence of needing to be
what others required.
And it wasn't this sense of space,
the chance to do as she chose –
yes, she enjoyed it,
looking forward to the galleries
and canals of Venice – the dank smells
and superb gilded horses of San Marco.
No, this sensation was like vertigo
or the stomach dropping into space
on a steep climb –
thinking of the man she'd meet.
It would be ordinary enough
but it would be her own, entirely,
not possessed by children
or the years that had smoothed her marriage
so that even arguments
had lost their heft.
She remembered it –

how once they'd been at loggerheads
for two days, and on the third, had made love
and had barely known each other
or themselves. She'd wanted to keep that –
the not-knowing, the animal life
that had risen. She had wanted
to stay strange to herself.

Paul Hetherington

The Capuchin

– Gran Lago, Nicaragua

I find him down by the boathouses,
a white-haired mystic with canine rhythm.
He paces and paces doggedly
and has a zoo look to his face.
His chain leads down from the soursop tree
to a pat of trodden mud and dung
where he guards a pool of runoff
and stares at his face in the gasoline.
He is a pet of one of the boatmen
whose blue and green covered craft
ferry tourists to Las Isletas.
I have travelled out there once
and seen his brethren
swinging high in the balsa trees.
In neat black caps and sheepskin
they hung like anvils in the flowers,
ministering deftly to each other
with fingers fine as Julieta cigars.
Like a penitent I approach him
and offer fruit to his terrible intelligence,
a few lime oranges from my bag
dropped into his calabash.
He turns his pink features to the sun
and shuns my offering, curling
his lyre-bird tail around the leash.
Here we are too far from the islands
and there is nothing I can do for him.
He looks at me with a mendicant air
and dips his paw into coconut cream,
then unhinges a long low howl on needled teeth.

His is the last true religion.
He practises sermons too green to transcribe
on the subject of the Sandinista revolution
to an early choir of sandflies,
then screams like the devil as the boats come in
and packs of gulls on the shoreline
carry on their cheerful scavenging.

Sarah Holland-Batt

The Humane Society

My mother brought home
the strangest creatures:
a lamb wearing a big white diaper;
a blind raccoon;
a wolfhound with a broken
hip, spooked by birthday balloons –

Then there was Mary Lou.
Two hundred sixty-five pounds and bruised,
she held a big leather purse,
drank diet pop,
smacked pink gum
and went to the movies alone.
Mother called her a Godsend.

Next, it was Lucy, a little girl
my mother gave violin lessons to
and called *daughter*.
Lucy wore her hair in a bob, took
over my old bedroom.
And then she moved
to sleeping next to my mother,
close to her under the covers
at night, holding her hand
in the big brass bed.

Soon mother kicked all of us out –
gave the seven sick cats
to my sister, found
my father a gritty flat, and took
his van keys. That's when she
brought home the man who beat her,
the Chinese man who broke her nose,
and pushed her all the way down
the shiny maple stairs.

Jodie Hollander

The Truffle Hunters

Dear mam last night
We drank a bottle of Tasmania
   I love you a lot only less so
      Pidgin monarch, belligerent fairy
Stone St Kilda the crone 'til she moves namore

We would waft 'cept for the human
     Gravity of density
Rich phlegmatic lungs of autumn belief
   The leaf's concerted flambé,
Black edg'd and separate
       Digitalia, heaped raunch
Impressionism as we were driven through
   By our pudgy headmistress, whom we tricked to admitting
'I want to be adored.'

Territory and plague :TA CHUANG
Vigorous strength, thunder, arousing heaven

   The rude tunics of the tiny army
Suck into the hollow
         Like degenerate dwarf song
Vespers of dusk come on – Monteverdi –
Where gods crawl through trumpets to get here
O mystery gizzrd,   O flunking west!
   O copper boned sopranos of Heidelberg!
Old French *superflueux* by my thin Red-
   thornproof hand

More than temples we'll have left
Wilderstrawberry   shits
                         Across Gaul
     My coo lipp'd rare
                    hipp'd Prospertine
I'm ovrly fond of the weeds where your street crosses
     my own   your original rigor pasted and pretty
                         as barbiturates
ride
isobars of clutching muscle
          that on odd days

ferry us to orgasm.

Duncan Hose

FUTURE HAPPY BUDDHA
vs Fake Kenny Rogers Head

Some people hang these crystals in their homes and cars.
This is called a cobra hood, you can do it silently.
MySpace, yes, Kenny and the Elephants, but who cares?
So these beads are pretty too.
I'm great and
I'm really interested to know you, FUTURE HAPPY BUDDHA.

A zinc finger homeobox transcription factor
acting late in neuronal differentiation:
fake Kenny Rogers Head. Macrobiotic, of course.
So if I was to dig up all these rocks,
I would find dirt on the bottom?
No, just fake Kenny Rogers Heads. All the way down.

D.J. Huppatz

The Frequency of God

At a trash 'n' treasure market,
in an average town,
an old radio
encased in bakelite.

Plugged in and
waiting for the valves to warm
I took to the dial with a frothing sense of urgency,
twisting past horse races and rock and roll,
past right-wing commentary,
      searching for the frequency of God,
long lost in digital audio,
      sure to be found
in the silver soldered
magic of a romanticised time.

      And there
at the end
of the amplitude modulated band,
        megahertz away from any generic noise,
      a perfect silence.

Mark William Jackson

Miracle on Blue Mouse Street, Dublin

for Leo Cullen who said: 'Once Celtic tiger Ireland; now no teeth!'

In a doorway from the rain, on Blue Mouse Street,
he was shouting 'Miracles! More miracles to come!'
The old beggar with the battered suitcase said,
'Yes, I am sure there will be one for you.'
So I walked over, closer to his sign, which said:
Miracles For Sale! Compact and Portable!

He spoke conspiratorially when he saw my coins.
'Come closer,' he said. 'To me, you look a little
worried, as if lacking air, or joie de vivre,
but are lucky anyway. Because I see my suitcase
is going to open for you, and believe that a miracle
might well come out of my suitcase. And I look forward
to knowing how this suitcase miracle will manifest
itself, as I am quite certain now that it will!
Now listen,' he said, 'and don't miss out.'

He took a plastic comb, held it to his mouth
and hummed and wheezed dreadfully through it.
'That tune is called "Our Happiness",' he said.
It made all the sparrows shake up from the trees.
And made small children run and cry, and the rain fall much
    harder.
He smiled, twirled and did a little hop and broken dance.

'I love my life,' he said. 'I love selling hope and miracles out here
in the rain, to all the passers-by on Blue Mouse Street.
Look,' he said, 'I have a pocket full of holes. These are my
    "loopholes",
and I pay no tax.' And he pulled his pockets inside out, and
    showed me.

'I had a pocket full of hope once, but hope or fine illusions,
or any sort of negotiable miracle, all being invisible,
weigh less than a suitcase I carry for a rainy day like this one,
always hoping for a miracle to manifest, for my paying public.
Look!' And I imagined I saw us both standing there,
just then, and something was moving. 'Yes, I believe
it is already starting to manifest, or snap open,'

he said. And the lid swung up and, inside the case,
I saw an old beggar open a suitcase. And inside that
was a smaller case, and us standing there, leaning
over a case that had just popped open, and so on …
but when I turned, he was gone, and so was the suitcase.
Only a muddy puddle where he had stood, but I could still
hear his tune, 'Our Happiness', wheezing faintly through the rain.

John Jenkins

Coal and Water

Now the last line won't irrigate
Dog-jawed ministers pant on camera
wan half-rhymes
filling dry channels
like droplets shaken from a child's flask
In tour-of-duty heat
a neat tie
may be a metaphor for resolution
If only the lack of a definite article
before 'country'
didn't make them stammer so
Meanwhile the press's compound eye
hallucinates a Chinese-invested coal station
mid-stream, when mid-stream is simply an illusion
of a liquid past
something the doctor asks you to save
in a bottle

Some poets have forgotten
to ask what it is
they are burning in the grate
On a cold night I am one of them
– the coal-fired heart
the pathetic revenge of the powerless
bringing paper fuel to the table
to burn and burn again
Is this all that's left?
The restive recitals
the pained nostalgia for trees and rivers
that comes *after* trees and rivers?

Contemplating this dun catalogue
makes me tired
as if I had walked
the salt bed of the Murray from north to south
dragging my plastic pen
through the silt like an ape

There is nothing I want to save in a bottle

A. Frances Johnson

Send in the Clowns

i.m. Peter Porter

You were the high-wire act,
me in my clown-suit on the slack-rope below.
We didn't appear much together in fact:
you in your eminence much the more famous show.
Still in the long times we met
we shared all our knowledge and taste,
talking around and around
about politics, art and music without haste
and would have done so for many a year
had you not fallen to the ground.
Send in the clowns?
          Don't bother, I'm here.

Evan Jones

Break on Through

I remember part of my bootleg
something boiling over
but someone still had
an eye on the game
the serene, small television
I was original mono
someone was singing
like milk happening
psychedelic ball pock bang
the dogs were touching
things with changelings
charged with damages
emptying the fire extinguisher
into the ash tray
I'm taking notes
then must sing them
expedition to a place
where I can think
the end being the apex
hypnotic sound from
someone's hands on
the vox turned low

I remember being
pulled down a road
I had to stop miming
my watch though
time keeps going
begins to end static
wires tubes and batteries
only present crackles
within the harmonium
and sublime's shaky hands
I was original bootleg
vox hypno and charge

Jill Jones

Triangulating the Tasman

(i) Warwick, NY
A point has no dimension: the bird in flight across the field
describes a line, but does not exist anywhere on that line.

The cardinal is a red point, the jay a blue.
Here, everything is contained in the immensity of the present.

When we leave for the airport, in anticipation,
with regret, we enter time.

(ii) Talbot, Vic
Atop our ancient volcano, we are cleansed by the heat
of January – pasteurised, as a poet put it.

The agisted sheep gnaw the ground, but the grass is eternal.
We name the mountains around us, ignorant of their true
    names.

The windmills to the southwest, the new horizon, have no
    names.
We do not want to leave here, which is the point of coming.

(iii) Kawhia, Waikato
In the afternoon, Carmen sits and drums on a log:
all the cows gather to watch her. We focus on this one moment.

What are the pearls on your necklace, the figures on your torq?
At the heart of travel is blood and family ties.

How much are you willing to pay for what you want?
In leaving, what we leave behind we hope is a gift, not a sorrow.

(iv) New York
'Get out of *my* terminal!' shouts the cop in JFK.
It's all street theatre here, and underneath, on the E line.

'What's the point of travel?' we ask. Three lines to three places,
only to do it all over again.

The red-tail hawk, with its speckled breast, makes one crashing
    dive
to carry off the sparrow on the railing.

How pointless can it be, when our lives describe a triangle,
while we find ourselves at home at the centre of ourselves?

Paul Kane

Rapptown

A jingle woke and gee-up knew.
Who prime-numbered the village –
routed the countryside? a wolf sack
filled with of courses, perhapses, and maybe.
Power feeds the organ's gaskets, postures,
lizard, plasma, shouting blue – schism –
people believe and behave. Where country
and town woe begone, the cars breathe fire.
There was relax and friend-hut, warmth
to the chilled the shelterer provided;
a gentle hand opened a door to the future
and the village? A nymph went wild – a guest's
wheels – then the bull exploded, the creek
flooded, the shower screen was brilliantine.

S.K. Kelen

Temporality

I'll ask you to assemble here
next to the step where so many feet have stood shifting,
waiting for a welcome,
that they have worn a cupped impression in the brick.

There are no headphones or podcast,
no virtual tour
nothing is animatronic
there are not even signs;
in this museum objects must be noticed
in order to be named.

Let me invite you
to put your sceptical fingers here, into a wall
cracked open like a seam;
in that arid subsiding spot,
with its bite of jagged mortar exposed,
feel the evidence, deliberate as a glacier,
of movement
of the power of slow ruin.

And in the shed on this salvaged beam
taken from the old factory, you can read
the faded names of workers from half a century ago
still scrawled, provisionally, in pencil:
Joe Wally Gavin Terry

This four-inch nail banged in beside them to hold invoices
that they always meant to replace with a decent hook or clip;
see how it's still holding fast
long after they have gone,
see how they were wrong
about what was temporary.

These are the exhibits worth naming,
the triumph of the nondescript
the steady rise and rise
of the inevitable.

Seeing them here, barely visible, demanding nothing,
might remind you of your own belongings –
the last things you expected to have bundled under your arm;
the shirts washed colourless, and the unfinished books
that you know would have done you good,
one hand clutching the dented pie dish, scored
like an endless unsolved equation
the hat with its forgotten tidemarks of sweat

everything it's too late to grieve for
that you thought you had discarded
everything you used, unthinkingly,
until it was burnished
into invisibility
these remnants, adrift from their stories,
will end up here too.

Whatever lies we tell ourselves,
these are the things that will outlive us:
that brick
will see us out;
that forgotten nail
driven in with four heedless, glinting hammer blows
back in 1957
will remain immoveable in that piece of hardwood
when you and I are dust.

And the ghosts who've stopped in this doorway
and rested one hand tiredly against the wall
to take off their boots before coming inside –
just here, their fingers grazing this worn unsanctified spot –
their voices are as distant
as impossible
as sirens.

Well, this is where I leave you
to make your way through the rooms,
threading back and back into the hushed corners,
your lips moving with recognition,
until there are no rooms
until you are standing empty-handed
in the sunlight.

Cate Kennedy

Expat

'The sun hit me in the face like a bully,'
wrote Laurie Lee in *Cider with Rosie*.
Our teacher, Mr Foster, said that was 'glib'.

Unfortunately, we didn't know what 'glib' was,
so Mr Foster had to explain,
and the more substantial point was pushed

to the back of the mind. Until today,
when, a quarter of a century on,
and resident in a foreign land,

I decided that he was probably right,
before dozing off with a drink in my hand,
the late sun blackening both my eyes.

Richard King

The History Idea

What's history? Is history
when Abraham Lincoln stands, thinking,
hand on the back of a chair?

Is history those breathless bludgeonings, the sporadic wild words
from the mist at Culloden?

What is history? Is it when everyone believes the handshakes
in spite of all the epaulettes?

Is it history when Picasso and his guests
see six pudgy German tourists
lying in a nude row on the cobbled beach
not far from Antibes, scrotums lined up
like apologetic mice,
like subdued
sausages?

The guests laugh
at these incongruous, privileged bodies –
but the painter frowns, remembering
carolling children's voices, footsteps of unsuspecting lightness,
the edicted morning school assemblies,
the boots of Nazis misunderstanding
Paris stairs.

Is that history?
The Nazis loved their music. Is that history?
Is history the steaming biosphere, water
lashing empty lanes? Is history present tense?

That's what history does –
it bites us, then looks away.

Graeme Kinross-Smith

It Begins with Darkness

People file into the room, find their seats,
fill up the air with chatter. The stage
is bare except for a leather couch
and a lamp on a chrome and bakelite stand.
It's meant to be an old factory converted
to an apartment – exposed pipes, a ceiling
fit for a cathedral, polished oak floorboards.
A man dressed in black makes an announcement
about mobile phones. The lights go down.
I don't know what I'm doing here,
I just know that this is theatre, my son an actor.

I hear his voice before I see him. It's as loud
as the wind swatting at a loose sheet of corrugated iron
on the chook shed. When he comes on stage
he swears five times in the first minute,
all in the presence of a lady. I've a good mind
to go down and slap him about the face,
except that I'm sitting right in the middle of the row
and it wouldn't be easy getting past all those knees.
Then I remember that he's pretending
to be someone else, that this is his job now.
Soon everyone is laughing – they're smiling
and nodding and taking in every move my son makes.

I've never been to a play before. It's not
boilermaking, not the flying sparks from an arc welder,
not the precision required for a submarine hull,
nor the relief of taking off your helmet,
gloves and apron and enjoying the coolness
of a harbour breeze as you eat your lunch,

but it is, I guess, a different kind of trade.
I watch more and it all happens before my eyes
and I can see that he loves this lady,
everyone can see it and I want to say, 'Son,
what are you afraid of?' I want to reach out
and lift him up as I did when he was two
years old, riding a supermarket trolley
and screaming as if he'd just discovered
the power of his lungs. But I can't touch him now
or even talk to him and I have this feeling
that it will turn out badly, like the week you have
the numbers in Lotto, but forget to buy the ticket.

The stage is dark again and he's not swearing now
and the lady's really pleased to see him
and she burns this scrap of paper and it flares up,
bright and yellow in the darkness
and the flame flickers across his forehead
and I glimpse in my son's face the unmistakable
features of my father who is ten years dead.
Although the three of us won't ever meet again,
I'm sure Dad would have loved this – a story
that takes a whole evening in the telling
and a small fire that leaps and glows
and transfixes us, for as long as it burns.

Andy Kissane

Mise en Scène

I dream the films I'll never make.
They have misty titles like
'Boy at a Window', 'Shadow of a Dog',
'Odalisque/Oblique'. They would play
short seasons in empty cinemas.
'Self Portraits' consists of fake after fake.
'Young Loves or the Fang of Time'
is shot with persistent, nostalgic lust
in black and white and blurs of poppy.
'South Coast Trilogy' has the distant haze
of over-exposure, of things long lost
that no longer matter, except to me –
flying sometimes, crawling sometimes,
from too much memory.

Mike Ladd

into the index

buy some strong alcohol at changi
but don't drink it

attractive face pileup

each feature a harbinger
it's eyes that wear uniforms

pinching those witnesses
from the picture

'what colour do you call that'

/

that's what my eyes call it

Sam Langer

Sydney and the Bush

In Sydney,
our absence is visible.

Most cities just fall away,
like a tale out of steam.

But Sydney abrupts to a light-cave:
a cavern of leaf-scrawls and glare.

High up, you get to subsume it: your *outlook*.

But down there and in it,
you hack through a bright lack of interest;
a steep disregard for potential, or goodness, or mood.

Mostly, we like to believe
there's a shore for each utterance.

But you can't always reach one. Not here.

Where the bush can pop up almost anywhere ...

It is why we're so smiley. And doubtful. And vaguely bereft.

No point in getting upset if there's nobody there.

And they're pretty as this.

Martin Langford

Quolls

Two x-rays of spotted quolls
flutter-slip into a wafer of sunlight in a clearing
where a National Parks ranger
pins the boned celluloid
to a viewing table of lit, woven grass
then stands back to assess the inner, carnivorous life.
She removes her greater glider mask
and the hairclip she's fashioned
from coral tree thorns.
There is blood on her wrist.
Under her gathered hair
her neck is redolent of an embrace
whose details are still alive in her
after thirty years.
The x-rays blow away
with a sound all transparencies make
when no longer useful.
A stopped cloud turns the scene
into a waiting room on a farm
inside the head of the husband
of a bipolar ranger.
Let it rain, darling, he says, with the kind of understanding
you sometimes find
in the eyes of wild animals, at close range
and it does rain, and for a very long time.

Anthony Lawrence

Unlicensed (from Spring Forest)

Unlicensed I drive along roads I know well,
in the same year
a widower and great-grandfather.
At dusk my mind takes a short walk
and visits
the burial place on a hill.

With the cattle gone
the land is coming back,
the ruined acres are restored.
Birds I've not seen for years
and perennial native grasses
are plentiful again,
and some interloper crimson roses
among blue wattle foliage and red clay
and dogs – my pet wolves – barking through chicken wire
are wet with the evening dew
of doing nothing.

We stood as a gramophone cranked out
'God Save the King'
then sat on a blanket and watched giant shapes
flicker on a sheet that billowed in the night.

My kin wore wide-brimmed felt hats.
We believed ourselves royalists
but acted like republicans.
We were pink Anglo-Celts who drove
a scattering of dark-skinned tribes from their titles.
We killed as they killed,
and the dead can't apologise.

I drink stolen water
and taste no contamination.
I conserve seeds and flowers and names.
But the world is not a museum – we are not curators.
The ballad's afterglow
is consumed by the future.

Geoffrey Lehmann

Sierra Nevada

i am Lew Welch hurrying
into the hills, vapid fumes of hope streaming behind me;
the entrails of an animal thought extinct.

the gun stashed
(not even my friends know i like guns, well they do now.),
but uncomfortable against my skinny ribs, elementally exposed.

rap rap rapid words
bubbling so furiously you could ride them
to the mountain top, if such a thing, you know.

And this damn gun.

the stars blinking on, the day slinking off.
the night welcoming; the salt earth
beckoning my tired bones and feet that
move independently as does that lizard's eyes.
i forget which, i forget which.

After all, this is just a story.

i am the silence hurrying
down the barrel, down the goat track,
i can't get there fast enough, (what
does it mean to disappear? tell me

that.)
the place i'll know or it will know; a
mutual concurrence of exhaustion,
singing like cooling rocks and beasts under the clear eyes
    of desert.

the names of these slopes and valleys
an unrequited love. (dimming now but methinks
that's just the light.) musical and terrifying. as if San Fran or
    Chicago never existed.
and why i took it or why it took me
as mysterious as the word
'posthumous'.

And then there's this thing the gun wants; an irrefutable quiet.

as if Lew Welch never existed.

W.M. Lewis

Crush

When I say that history was my favourite
I'm thinking less of the Weimar Republic
or the militarisation of Japan
than Miss R's contralto discipline
and her homemade Chanel suits.

For her I spend my afternoons
between the light blue covers
of the Cambridge History of England.
Pendant mes vacances
my special project is Eleanora Duse.

When she asks if she can keep it
I am nonchalant as hell.

Kate Lilley

Bodies of Pompeii

It is not the delicate detail, for the cast is too crude
for that: this girl's face obliterated by weeping plaster,

a man's extremities reduced to rounded stumps. It is
the large arrested gesture that tells these bodies, saying:

So this is the shape of death. Familiar lovers fastened
on a stone bed (whereas life might have ripped them apart),

a dog's high-pitched contortion, an entire family sleeping,
the baby rolled absently from its mother.

Unburied, they weigh more than bone ever could.
They have shaken off the ash and refuse to rest. So many

stopped limbs. Mouth holes, eye holes, a balled fist.
But in the end, this is what halts you: how a young woman sits

with her knees drawn up to her chest, hands covering eyes.
How a child's body folds, alone at the final moment –

and a man rises from his bed, as if waking for the first time.

Debbie Lim

5.30 a.m.

It's 5.30 a.m.
God and I stand
on the verandah.
I'm surprised to see
him smoking a pipe.
'I don't do the drawback,'
he says. His corduroy trousers
are the colour of wheat-stubble
and the deep pockets of his moss-green
cardigan exude an earthy smell.
His voice seems to rise
out of his pipe-smoke
as he asks how I like the morning.
I tell him that the rosy glow
hovering on the horizon
reminds me of the liquor
I got when I poached
the white peaches last summer.
He sucks on his pipe and nods.
'What are you on about?' I ask.
He stares at the limpid sky.
The pipe gently ignites.
A puff of smoke ascends
and becomes a cumulonimbus.
'Looks like rain,' he says.
'You'd better go in.'

Helen Lindstrom

Lovetypes

I speak of love in one pan; love for potatoes
love in a tablet, love and debts or sermons.
I mistook pleasure-giving for a seedtext –
two cowboys and a pickaxe – sheepdogs
nudging ewes for a droplet. Needleworking
guts as a cat lopes, a cat disappears like a dumb seed
nosing into the folds of a sheep's fleece. A cat
is in love, in love with Russia, with minerals and
rivers. The way we love borders. The way we
learned to love physics, the way we used to
love globalisation. THE WAY WE LOVE
TECHNOLOGY! Loving difference or Buddhism.
Pornographic or scatological loves at odds with
chance. Love so slovenly, so clumsy. I love it and
I tell it. I abandoned illiteracy as untrustworthy.
Sew up the sheep's neck with stitches where it
was bitten by an overachieving dog, you will find
that the neck tastes as catnip, a zone for loose and
metallic thinking, stretched out, guts airing.
Someone's gonna read this, this love like police presence.

Astrid Lorange

In the Laneway

And voices come over the back fences, and the *phttt phttt phttt*
of the sprinkler throwing out streamers of crystals
past the bleached wooden posts
into the shadows
on the cracked path of the laneway.
The shadows are from the trees in the backyards
– there are no trees in the lane –
only tufts of grass between the cracks
and here and there, a yellow daisy
in the windless half-light. If you stretch your neck
you can just see the lucky people in the backyards.
They laugh in the sunlight, the wind lifts their hair,
their clothes are bright squares of colour.
But the ache in your neck means
you cannot strain for long; you drop back
to the hot dirt and look through the shadows
to where the lane rises into a darkness you've never noticed.
You walk past the yards, past entire lives lived
while you were sleeping, toward the slow murmur of the others
at the end of the laneway. But everyone who matters
is further ahead or hasn't arrived. And you wonder,
Was all that writing about the dead a game? As the last crystal
    drop
disappears without a trace in the dirt at your feet, was it real
or was it a dream?

You wonder, Is the dirt at your feet real? The last crystal drop
disappearing without a trace must be a dream. Maybe
while you were sleeping, everyone who mattered
arrived and went further ahead.

If you walk past the slow murmur from the backyards,
you will surely find the others at the end of the laneway
beyond the rise where the shadows drop into darkness.
You cannot be bothered straining to look into the lives
of the people in their hot backyards: many will be sleeping. Why
stretch your luck when the world here has so many bright
     squares
of colour: tufts of grass, a yellow daisy. It is odd
the way the dappled shadows shift across the cracks:
there are no trees in the lane.
The windless half-light lies down
on the cracked path. And the stream of pale crystals that wet
the bleached wood posts are unstrung in the laneway. They fall
and are still as the sprinkler goes *phttt ... pht ... tt ... ph ... t ... t*
and the voices over the back fences stop.

Roberta Lowing

Sonnet

The hills arrived and I kept driving.
With every civic car park this theory
Of joint tenancy grew more abstract.
There were shared passwords
And beds unmade with abandon,
But I didn't want to ruin
Our argument with the past.
Citing roadkill would be callow
So I sent back cards
Left blank for your thoughts.
I counted ructions
And the miles between them.
Where the road withered
Lay a Switzerland of the heart.

Anthony Lynch

(Weldon Kees)

Everything is ominous.

–

Another ordered loneliness.

–

The future is fatal.

–

Even the open field, a labyrinth.

–

The afternoon idly flicks through the pages of itself.

–

A list of names: good news, or bad?

–

The long silence of rooms.

–

History with its morphine headache.

–

The anonymous rain falling on motels.

–

The atrocities played under flickering streetlights.

–

The cars parked under melodramatic weather.

–

Finally, every future is fatal.

David McCooey

Grandfather

Began my search in middle-age: for the drunk with florid face
    gazing
from a grainy photo. First your gravesite, words wearing
away from the slippery stone both smooth and blanched.
    Website

offering wartime records touted the existence of medals
that would never be recovered. Verified you married in London
and brought home the bride. During the war you were court-
    martialled

for insubordination, often arrested on premises out of bounds.
But gambling dens or brothels? I don't know which. My mother
    supplied
some snippets: knowledge barely covering thirty minutes

– let alone those thirty mislaid years. Your brick-making trade
    demolished
by the Depression, you chased jobs you could seldom grasp,
    scampered
from house to house before landlords clobbered you for their
    rent.

Your only sport, the Australian Crawl through an ocean of
    booze, cascading
down the bars of Adelaide's public houses. Loss of an eye
    laying pipes provided
compensation, and furniture finally arrived for the family.
    Furniture

my mother had only seen on the cinema screen. Your wife at
    forty died lonely
and homesick in this foreign land. Ironically, from a weakened
    heart
– though most conceded it had really been broken.
    Disintegration

of immediate family followed, then the dalliance with a sodden
    neighbour.
And I was puzzled by your urgent quest for a life in the west,
    only to return
and die painfully, a few months later. I questioned and
    researched

but found no account of this time: where you went, what you did.
    And the one
who might have remembered has now joined you on the other
    side. Rumours filtered
down your new wife was killed by a car after visiting your grave.
    But she left

no death certificate, nor paper trail I could follow. It's as if she
    vanished
with the remainder of your whisky-stained notes, and drowned
    herself
in a billabong of booze in some obscure corner of your
    tarnished empire.

David McGuigan

Late Night Shopping

It is late at night when the Primitives emerge.
They withdraw their cash and go marketing abroad.
Strung with small hard parcels Malice rushes in.
She joins Obsession, Hate, Revenge.
They fuss about dressed in puce, red, yellow.
They stay their hand and while they prevaricate
Doubt sidles by without a word.
Panic takes off and hails an outbound bus.
Anxiety tries it on for size but rarely buys –
The price is never right and she can't negotiate.
Fear's on a bargain hunt but stuffs the whole deal up.
They will not seize the hour –
Uncanny, unlucky bedfellows.

Rhyll McMaster

A Great Education

(When asked if there was an example who had inspired her as Dietrich Bonhoeffer inspired Kevin Rudd, Julia Gillard replied 'Nye Bevan')

Aneurin Bevan woke up in flat Bathurst, to the drone
of Julia Gillard's 'Ben Chifley, Light on the Hill'
speech as she condescended that Chifley
always regretted his lack of 'a great education'.
Bevan had left school at thirteen, self-taught proudly
like Chifley. He wondered if Gillard ever knew
the power of freely chosen knowledge. When young,
he'd detested that chainstore quality he called
'Everything in its place and nothing above
sixpence.' She liked 'universality of education', her faith
in uniforms startling to a man who thought
socialism meant avoiding them, her stress
on educational achievements hollowly passim
insisting one acknowledge all her own. He thought
of Chifley and Evatt roasting baked potatoes
on a Murray houseboat, each free of envy
of the other's erudition. Then his irritation
became pity when he pictured Gillard
Welshly stiff in a little uniform, Welsh-mam-bossy
like his own mother, or nervously flirty, that old anxiety
of women for respect in crisis leaping
at their throats like blazer emblems,
unable to orate as he had: to think swiftly
on the spot, as his hand pressed on his heart.

Jennifer Maiden

Snake Lady

Over the fence my newest neighbour greets me
swathed in her pet python (green and gold:
a good two metres). Never in a million years
could I pick up a thing like that. I've always had
an absolute horror of snakes of any kind.
Go on, she says, he'll let you stroke him.
Her hair twines down in ringlets, dark and sinuous.
I stroke him. He feels like a rather expensive handbag.
The snake lady's arms are silken and not like a handbag at all.

John Miles

Claustrophilic Lavallière

You were too good to cry much over me.
And now I let you go. Signed, The Dwarf.
                    —JOHN ASHBERY

I'm presuming, I know (just as winter will
unite enemies in spring, betray soporific words
left a tiny bit unhingd &, all gilt, such paroxetine
somnolence weakly ornamented – I thought
error might better pass enclosd, your coercion
somewhat sluiced by a subigated rose, an ouevre's
brocaded recitations, garlands left dishevelled
in the fog; my foliate despair (a locket) shows
(ingenious as mind-control ordaind by queer cherubs)
a Sun King smiling radiant while drawing
unself-conscious blancs from her morphine powderd
throne, an asthenic coterie (kept glad of work!)
laying about the cruel enclosure with studied
cartouchés, eyelids clasping inlaid silver birds.

So, the reason why I right up Verse, ills aside,
and carry charmd totes inside this bird of paradox,
informants gushing tedious and jocund, is, honey,
instrumental – the republic, enamelld & reductive,
its interiors' consigned affiliations, slops of law
and capital's bulbous, cordial seductions
grant lip service to this beguiling inheritance
(materialist, undetermin'd, in arrears) common sense
depository and melamine; *Wallpaper* faces
unletterd & besmirchd by mismated possibility
drift across the onerous couch, a city wakes bedazzld
by the birth of a gildd, stirrupd fricatrice.

The reason for this mise en scène is, you know
'cause we live like worms) & think to like it.

Peter Minter

Going to the City,
Karachi 2010

As the tractor-exhaust
vistas of desert sky
resume the south ahead
the farmer and his family
are moving to the city

in debt and crusted cloth
at the river's speed
close but not together
going and reappearing
under the raft of noon

moving to the city

Les Murray

Reading Laurie Duggan in the Shanghai New Zhen Jiang Restaurant

If only I spoke Mandarin
like a peasant, I'd say to the waiter
who compliments my crap Hanzi
copy of the restaurant name, 'I could do better
if only I had prepared'
(great deathbed confessions: if only ...).
I'd take my time,
learning how to speak like a child
and not pretend. Great translations
take gall and humility in equal measure.
I feel like putting up my hand
and asking for an extension
or another serving of the eggplant dish.
Meanwhile, Laurie is hacking into Les again;
downstairs, a banshee scream
of a little emperor thwarted.
'It's death,' my aunt says, 'and he's
reading your poems.'
Frank Sinatra sings 'unforgettable'.

David Musgrave

Thursday April 21. Canberra

A raven, half a grove of poplars after wake
one receives news that one is gone
morse calls, toll calls and black
I stand on the ground of the displaced, scything the tufts
dawn bells – mathematical series of grey, and shades
after deaths.
Old People's House washed over with chinawhite fineness
art deco lines and the never-never-mind
a fire, left overnight, burnt to ground, wisps
cataract sky hanging low with a few decoys
one that was my father's ghost
on the mindsets of the villagers, his kin.
Of calligraphy, a word wrested
itself out of the mace of a young monk
wrote itself a wing and pressed hard a final dot
on the floor of the freshly dug grave, soft as flesh –
goodness returns to goodness – lush waves of wild grass rolling.
Under faded clouds, grains of my childhood
now I enter a Greek Orthodox house of worship in Kingston
swim in the rising tongues
of islands and archipelagos and the upturned seas
bathed in a hologram, sun washing over years and feet
held in caring hands, then
cut, roped, shifted, hanged up, nailed, in, out, under, over
dirt – warm, ever so, breathing

Nguyen Tien Hoang

Values Meeting

Down there by the fence is where everybody goes
to have sex.   Back to first nothingness,
a soapbox shouting, its own goalkeep,
scores, falling into conception: to posit

the use of fire as a universal right ... a different
coat of arms for each insect.
But how combine
individual responsibility with a sense

of community, as the tone, fine-tuned, combines
brightness and power? See, this
is just the discussion we've been needing
to have, like, do we believe in love?   & if God is love,

- maybe we should be worshipping him?
- & if so, in what way precisely?

       ←
       ←
       ←
       ←

Jal Nicholl

Our Lady of Coogee

Turning it over
it's no coincidence
that the famous Tom Roberts painting
Holiday sketch at Coogee, 1888
preserved here in postcard form
is also the same view of the very fence post
where Christ's mother appeared to the people of Coogee
on those heated, sunstruck afternoons.

In the painting no one on the beach is nude.
People stroll the shore under parasols.
Cliffs in the distance, minus bathing baths.
Impressionism captures haze so well.
No shark has vomited up a tattooed arm in the aquarium.
No distant world wars. Not even a ravenous gull.
No cynical fence post, either, to deflect
the sunbright glare of Coogee's vision splendid.

It is as if the figure that might be Our Lady (dressed
in black) is picnicking,
surveying distant figures across the hot sand.
The sky beautiful as a bruise,
the waves petrified tulle frozen in paint.

Yet motion is what's wanted
as Our Lady of Coogee finally stands up,
black as pitch,
brushes crumbs from her holy shroud
amidst the fish and chip wrappings,
the apparition's vandalised fence post,
and opens her arms in wonder
at the miracle of real estate.

Mark O'Flynn

Four Thirteen

kicking in windows like old tvs
lasso some hose to scatter stray
hosts of morning tv, the kind
who're evangelical about anything

the day began with the question
of how to fold the labour
– simultaneous declaration
    of necessary breeze –

suburban magnolia puts on a show
'on you frills lose their cuteness'

our street lacks verticality
    thus becomes a drive by

optimistic housetags
e.g. call it
FLORIDA
    & the cubist palm trees
        will grow in Moonee Ponds

living close to the tracks
just to know things are going
(or that you can get going)

these things that are the same as
looking at your own handwriting

go upstairs to practise baton twirls,
a double-hander flag routine
     & other choreographed delights

radio waves stirring the pond
where ducks collect surface dross
switching easily between
     air & gelatinous water

with an eye to the cinematic
a swan lands gracelessly
     spraying mud, bits of weed
          but making me think of a version of Zeus
     as rendered by Rubens
        (all white feathers pressed
             indecently on creamy thighs)

poor Leda not yet
     hip to the ruse

Ella O'Keefe

Reconfigured

So when I went out of the bathroom I knew that no one was
   there.
So I went out naked, dripping wet, it didn't matter.
So I was surprised when I was decapitated by the ceiling fan.
So I was upset when I was castrated by the bread knife.
So it was very hard to understand when I was disembowelled by
   the corkscrew.
When the television curled up inside my vacant abdomen,
it was not only extremely uncomfortable but it was also
   incredibly hard to watch the six o'clock news.
Only then did I realise my error in purchasing at a heavily
   discounted price the wide screen TV that was all the fashion.

The linoleum spinning, coiled round my feet, I tripped and fell.
Retarded, I threshed on the floor raising weeks of unswept dust
curling up in hurricanes, gouging emptiness into the walls.
Disturbed cockroaches fled in plagues to the safety of my only
   safe earlobe
with a flower pot hanging metallically by an ear-ringed
   mutilation.
The abdominal TV was vomited in my terror through a torn
   oesophagus
while its news presenter sprayed litres of insect spray on the
   forty-thousand cockroaches nestling cosy by my eardrum.
Only then did I notice that I could not notice what I noticed
   because the notice was pinned far away in the kitchen on
   the fridge.

The kitchen, my enemy, scalded me with its water, burnt me
    with its stove
and soaked me in the chatter and clatter of frying pans and
    saucepans.
Sugar stirred cunningly in every sweet delight in the pantry
in an unflattering eagerness to rush me into a diabetic extreme.
The power of the fatty food and the lure of the lounge
sent me spiralling into inaction, baldness and middle age,
severed from my reality by an unkind addiction to a
    comfortable life in a suburban brick and tile lawn-mowed
    masquerade,
in a piteously unwanted prosthetic of a globally embedded city,
    flamboyant in fashion's leading skirts.

And the notice, it went coldly, refrigerated as it were in
    temperatures Antarctic.
It told me its ol' story, flapping beneath a dreary plastic
    butterfly magnet:
buy some milk, put the cat out, duck when the ceiling fan spins,
sweep the floor, spray the cockroaches, mow the lawn,
avoid the knives and the corkscrew and don't turn on the TV.
I replaced my head and my balls, and other bits and pieces
    wherever they fitted best.
I coerced the TV back to its allotted place, and pontificated to
    all household items to be reconfigured to suit the decor.
So I went back into the bathroom naked, dripping wet, it didn't
    matter, I knew that no one was there.

Paul O'Loughlin

I love

I love work even on weekends particularly on weekends
I love work on holidays
I love work after making love after eating a good meal after
    drinking a good drink
I love work trying to let other things rake my brains
I love work even when I am with people who talk rubbish
I love work even in sleep even when I am in a dream even
    when the dream sweats me
I love work making people happy making people forget me
I love work right back to the seventies right back to the fifties
    right back
I love work in deepest pleasures my mind bent to its inner
    curve
I love work when night straightens its back and stands
I love work filling the gaps of fallen teeth
I love work seeding the future with an irretrievable me

Ouyang Yu

The Red Gurnard

Silence is argument carried on by other means
—CHE GUEVARA

Against an outgoing tide
he comes up sluggish and sideways
like a reluctant *No*,

breaks the surface
and spins under my arm,
his shocked skin flashing orange.

There is only unhinged mouthing
and raised hackles; his panic
is a slow internal bleed.

I know who he is:
shape-shifter from a life
with other rules for beauty,

for movement and sensation;
a wet and breathless life.
We're spellbound:

I only have eyes for his eyes,
black from the grottos,
his faltering fins,

his undersea sail in tatters,
his sequined sides,
his crown of spines.

Kiss me now, he says,
his argument perfectly formed.

Louise Oxley

A Manual of Style

for Bernie McGann

Gruff at times but not ill-mannered

A hint of old-time dancing but
      the flattened fifths as well

Laconic, yes, but savage too

Angular, with no glass broken

Sad though far from sentimental

Aged but never out of date

Metallic but with friendly alloys

Unique but straight on down the strait

Legato, yes, for preference
      but still there at the turns.

The low notes hoarse the high no less so

Harmony remembered and euphony forsworn

The late-night book of smoky clichés
      always pushed away

Minor third without the third
      as T. Monk used to say

Geoff Page

'This is the Only Place…'

THIS IS THE ONLY PLACE I'VE EVER HEARD ANYONE
PLAY THE SOUNDTRACK FROM GHOSTBUSTERS sadly
my dad is not rapping in hebrew with his rainstick, it just sits
there next to the pile of newspapers we have … i spent good
money on that thing, do you want bubblegum for your cough?
████ is cute & we have fought twice, which isn't bad. (both
times about her mobile.) my results were ok, but not perfect.
there is a castle here. grandma is convinced a MUSLIM woman
is cutting the heads off her gardenias. she is covered in a layer
of what appears to be fine dust. or ash. perhaps i'm a marxist?
this is not like ████ coming out in one he was the bigfoot & he
& neil diamond were selling an album they've made on garage
band i went to see kevin johansen play for a second time.
drunk a lot of mate. haven't got a job. today i helped a man
catch his runaway donkey. but i had better start from the start,
everything else in tokyo seems to be just as good as

their toilets, it's weird to be in a place with no bogans
tomorrow we're going to disneyland! my boss watched
centrestage … she tell me to write this movie … i want a nice
bed linen … i loved so much to stay the wife … i want that
here in japan i am an old man. & you are a beautiful chicken.
CONGRATULATIONS!!!!!! this marks one week without
an infection. no pus for you! we are professional blueberry
pickers. we are now professional apple pickers. sorry for my
lacadazeical approach & spelling of lackadazecal

i am the quote dirty dirty child who doesn't succeed & hasn't made the movie of the year. love, john-hair-implants-didnt-work-galliano o i think i can be famous ... but i feel tired ... please lets go shopping i miss you like it is winter here.

Eddie Paterson

Ripples under the Skin

See the people crying in the streets.
The streets are rivers. They're jumping in.
Who is there calling?

See the ripples under the skin,
the terrible truths, the people's houses
tumble into the waves, their children
on the window sills, food still on the table.

The people aren't ready. They're still
in the uncurling, in a scene dark and
beautiful.

Janette Pieloor

Cyclone Plotting

The danger is that we'll drink this *one quick drink* too fast. The
danger is that one vodka beckons, flirting, to the next. The
   danger
is that, catching vodka's white wave, I could spill, purple. The
   danger is
that I will become a nest of Matryoshka dolls, falling out of
   myself. The danger is that
your umbrella, stripping its black veils one by one, will spoke
   my eye. The
danger is that the rain, hard, will fill the streets with people,
   pushing. The danger
is that with the smallest shove I'll miss my train. The danger is
that your every gesture, like a Cocteau film, must be
   deciphered. The danger is that
if I'm not lifted out of this hot storm everything will open,
   slippery and roof-shaking.
The danger is that I have invented you, and your hip bumping
   mine promisingly. The
danger is that the rain will wash away my lightning-flash
   glamour. The danger
is that you feel my softening. The danger is that you know it
   already. The danger is
that my rained-on hair cannot pretend to be a satin sheet.
   The danger is that
the only umbrella I have is paper, crimson and stuck in my
   third drink.

The danger is that I am well out of my depth in this gutterless
        downpour. The
danger is that you feel the mercury's rise and rise. The danger
is that you don't feel its rise, retaining your leather-jacketed
        cool. The danger is
that I am making this up out of nothing. The danger is that.

Felicity Plunkett

Misreading

I'll say how it's done so the difficult questions can be leavened
into small loaves of bread given in praise of crows.

Let's start at the beginning: under a perilous sun she wore
medallions of clear plastic, pom-poms of summer grass;
I wore fretted blues and feathered kneepads so our scuffle
precluded my bruised knees.

It is true I ripped her earring out which looked more dramatic
than it was.

She did hit me first, by the creek and the single willow
and after that, to my mind, she no longer resembled an orchid.

       So yes I pushed her flat into the dirt of this
difficult country; and it is true that I write as I read –
mistaking wreaths for wraiths, spires for spines, girls for orchids

Claire Potter

Cute

*… the cute and loving appreciation of my book and me
by them in Australia has gone right to my heart.*
　　　—WALT WHITMAN *writing to Bernard O'Dowd, 1891*

i wish to specifically send remembrances & love to you
& how is your mother bernard is she well? i do hope so

(tho i've never met her or your good self nevertheless
send her my regards & tell her to water the daisies often

& fred woods is well? i do hope the bruise heals soon
(tho what happened to him i can't tell either no matter

& young jim hartigan is he likewise well? i do hope so
but please do send him my best regards & the solution

to this week's crossword is enclosed ada i do hope she's
well you speak so highly of her i wonder whether she's

not your real wife after all now don't go jumping to
conclusions bernard i can only go by what you tell meh

about your bowel movements bernard are they regular
i pray so for you know my views on this issue prunes &

buttermilk (enough said eva i presume she's well oh
i hope so & as i know oh she's very cute in that photo

you mentioned enclosing never did arrive unfortunately
still i see her pretty well from here & very cute she is

& her parents mr & mrs fryer are both cute i hope so
please also kindly pass on to dear mr fryer my sincere

congratulations on winning the bridge tournament &
don't ask how i know! tell ted he's wanted in several

states over here (i'm sure he'll get the joke it's private
i don't recall who louie is but please send him or her

fond salutations & finally tom touchstone who i can't
place (no i'm getting nothing but suppose & hope he

is well i guess that's all but hi also to other friends not
named e.g. pet cats the milkman (oh he is a cute one

David Prater

How we tell stories about ourselves

It's a road you recognise from a car ad. What's it like to live here,
do you think, driving the same winding stretch every night,
waiting on set – that is, at home – for your thirty seconds
between snatches of *Law & Order*? And how do places
become redolent with stories, I wonder, what do they tell
about us?

We're already back at the house, though, drinking coffee as
morning mist drifts past. We flip a coin to decide who's taking
the kids to soccer and who's going to the beach with our young,
loosely clothed friends. They remind me of evangelists, the
    way they
perform without being prompted, sipping coke, laughing,
    having a great
time. Later, while you get grass stains out of the whites and I
knock together a no-fuss dinner, all I can think about is
    fucking them,
like, really going at it, real rough, dirty sex.

I need to go for a walk, step outside the frame,
marshal my resources. I think about when we bought our first
    house,
or got our first newspaper subscription (I can't remember
    which),
and it's apparent, even then, that things were already breaking
down. And so projecting forward, we can only wait to see
our hearts breaking, be recast, lose sight of what matters.
    There were no
simpler times, it turns out, no house by the beach. I don't
    recognise
anything now, much less tell stories or go driving, but
whatever happens, I look forward to looking back on this
    moment.

Aden Rolfe

Cicerone

Now is the time for the crucial chandelier.
Choose an hour when no one else is there,
the heat intense, the couturiers gone away.
Lead me down a circuitous route
barely speaking, the better to anticipate.
Part the leathern doors and introduce me
to the obscurest church ever visited.
Teach me about its forked history,
how it was bombed and rebombed
and sulkily rebuilt.
Point out the seminal chandelier
with its thousand-year-old brass
flung into the Tiber in a vandal's pique.
Indicate each notch on the ruined pulpit,
the mincing lion and indignant unicorn.
Move ahead of me into the sacristy,
remarking on a particular cerement.
Reveal each nuance of your classic neck.

Peter Rose

Quote

Outside
There's a dragon wind

A man comes to give a quote
For the dead trees
He clears his throat

I think he is going to go with Proust
'Your soul is a dark forest'
Or Gibran (popular
At weddings and funerals):
'If you reveal your secrets to the wind
You should not blame the wind
For revealing them to the trees'

Instead he tells us
Two thousand
Two hundred
Cut to the ground

Penni Russon

Daphnis and Chloe

He rides a Segway through the topiaried hedges
of the Institut pour le Développement Harmonique
Next it's granite and a TV spin-off
while she squirms in the scullery, an emulsifier
and a theodolite on each hand
when in Preston she crossed a ditch of sobs

She gathers the covenant to heart, before it lobs
her followers. Thought sledges
a wicket, but whether from glee or a stand
against corruption, who knows, a fit of pique
may as well summarise. She blogs: a death-defier
He pails water from a trough

parting a fence's palings with finesse, a cough
whistles. The demonstration magnifies her probs
and immanence, an astrolabe warped like a tyre
falls across some scratched ledgers
that yearn to annotate and squeak
of her chlorophyll, but awfully fanned

cards gloat and claim the land
was swamp. All bets are off
Return to the campfire: its clique
substitutes logs for chairs and sprigs for knobs
a saddle supporting her head edges
its cinders, i.e. the remains of a local flyer

promoting the environment, as if what they require
could ever class a gluey saraband
over dinner of fried wedges
He resumes the inspection, with Prof.
at an elbow, advising how to maximise jobs
and measuring exactly where the fountains leak

Whirr of helicopter off screen, over to Seek
.com. Either that or the National Choir
warbling probity, while an overseer dobs
her in. His wistful Peter Pan'd
check a rabbit fence will slough
the paddocks, while sunset's pink valve ceases pledges

– all Greek to her, she dredges
up some prior ownership, he bobs
among the damned, all the usual stuff

Gig Ryan

The Faces of the Unpunished

The trouble is they look so ordinary.
No tattoos no stubble and no concealed weapons
tucked into the belt
spoil the cool immaculate hang of their suits.

These Brahmins of the caste
system we shouldn't call a market it sounds
like the butcher and fishmonger and smells
off. The suits rob us of millions without

a single cop car screeching to a stop
(no melodrama, no bullet-proof vests).
The workers walk out into the too-real sun
and the directors pay themselves off

surreal millions, their features unremarkable
as if money erases them, and indifference keeps
them young. Not public signs for us to consider
these faces no one can bring to mind.

Philip Salom

Mr Habitat Delivers a Speech to the Lapidarists

One day, eventually, no escaping,
I give a speech – special guest
at the podium: stress. Gem
of an audience, a convention
of lapidarists. Hot, I broke open
the topic.
                  What was the problem?
I'd rather have been lost among rocks,
fractures and folds, than found
formally dressed, among strangers.
Exposed. They sat like fossils.
I gripped the podium as if
on a cliff, troubled there
by vertigo. Spoke. It was something
of a lava flow. My only hope
to cling to the script, stay cool
in the face of stony ridicule.

I'm flowing now, as if the video
won't leave me alone, the footage fresh
with my quaking. I go
along with the painted tribesmen, sad
to have their spirits stolen
by a rigid cameraman ... walked
away from surprise applause, pocketed
their gift: a polished trilobite.

Give it, at home in my warm palm
– wide of any seismic likelihood –
a reception better honed
only in the Cambrian explosion.

Andrew Sant

The Place in Darkness

What is it he's after – that book he lent you,
that tie left behind in your wardrobe?
Does he think you'll change your mind?
What is it he's after, this close to nightfall
and no lights on in the house –
bruising his knuckles on your door,
and you not about to answer.
He'll get sick of it, wait and see.
I admire your easy dismissal, glad
I'm not bruising mine.

You settle yourself back on me.
Hard, under the warmth of your skin,
to imagine being out in the cold,
standing on the other side of the door
with only your anger to hold.

Michael Sariban

January

for Peter Gizzi

We sit to a bowl of miso ramen,
same as the night before, only this time
you're coming down with something
and need the chilli. Later we'll sketch
a brief history of *risk*, the word's
first appearance in a seventeenth-
century translation of the Lusiad,
the Portuguese retelling of Homer
with da Gama as Odysseus; how
mortality data drawn from the plagues
in England gave birth to actuarial
science, and Halley, of comet fame
crunched the numbers for the seeds
of life insurance – the epistemic
shift from the providential view
that meant you'd sooner sacrifice
a goat before a trip than trust in
numbers. These days we rationalise:
what's the probability of the plane
falling out of the sky? You're far
more likely to be struck by lightning.

Did I tell you my father died in a plane
crash? you'll say, and I – mortified
by my hypothetical, nodding as you
explain your penchant for Xanax
on cross-Atlantic flights – think back
to this moment, ladling miso into
our mouths, steam rising in winter,
you explaining how you nursed
your dying mother this September
and muttering, half under your breath:
Dying is so expensive in America.

Jaya Savige

On the Up & Up

an giv my best
ta y'r missus
he ends his mobile

trying to sell
something –
insurance
cars
ice cream
   it doesn't matter

the world makes sense
to him

flitting around
the c.b.d.
asking
   urging
      selling

the smart ones
will tell you

it's all just energy

they won't tell you
about the intelligence
behind it

that stolid
ruthless
poison.

Mick Searles

Georges Perec in Brisbane

With the slums of Paris as the norm
Of course Brisbane is exotic.
Imagine ripe mangos dropping on your roof
Or the insistent flight of flying-foxes
Every evening. Humidity
Could be midsummer anywhere
Particularly mid-continent. It will pass.
Growth – not human – is what matters.
Humans are peripheral here
Whereas they are all that matters in Paris.
Life might be something to use;
Here it does not count. Insects
Have as much claim: they are everywhere.
It is strange to feel so isolated.
Do I feel something is wrong? No.
Everything has its own proportion
But I will go back to what I think of as home
And in ten months I will think of mosquitoes
As the improbable cousins of humanity.

Thomas Shapcott

Heroes of Australia

In bedrooms of Australia they are waking up and saying
What did I say and you know you should have stopped me and
My god did I say that and saying never that's the end of it no
    more
I'm giving up and swearing off it while their heads are full of
    saucepans
falling endlessly to floors made out of steel

And they are wearing cast-iron turbans that are growing ever
    smaller
round their temples while the stereo bangs on: it's descant
    sackbuts,
Philip Glass and Chinese Air Force marching bands and
    whining voices
Is that mine? that try to surface through the note-sludge and
    the chord-swamp
saying that's the end I know don't try to talk to me it hurts

The second last drink always is the one that does the damage
    what
possessed me to announce I love these cocktails I could drink
    them
all night long, or who says cask red wine's so rough let's have
    another
this is fun, it's Penny's big night out, it's Roger's last day with us
let's make sure we all remember while the café staff are
    laughing
looking on and counting money thinking ambulance or police

They're waking up and cannot face the ugly thing that's in the
    mirrors
that will catch them with its mug the simulacrum of a plastic
    drink cup
crushed, its two small pissholes in the snow glued somewhere
next to burst capillaries' cadastral lines around what was a nose
and will those tom-toms never cease

they're waking up if this can be called waking up instead of
resurrection from the dead and hearing noises coming out of
    furry caverns,
burred with algae, fungus, vacuum-cleaner sacks of dust and
    ashes
blurred with single malts and rotgut saying who's a clever boy
and who's a clever clogs and whimpering I know
I didn't mean it while massed choirs shout You did

Across the bedrooms of the nation they are crying o my god
    and omigod
and omg and g almighty Christ on earth and on a bicycle what
    happened
where was I when that truck hit me and I thought among this
    blasphemy
my misery must end why are you with me if not helpmeet,
    friend
to guide me through the labyrinth of sin, disgrace and worse,
    insult
my colleagues and employer and I have to leave for work now

They are speaking when they finally untie the Windsor knot
    that was
their tongue and making words out of the alphabet that's
    mixed up

saying Gertrude Steinways stone me, and the crows and all the
    raptors
Nevermore-wise as they hold their safety razors and attempt to
    shave
the hairs of dogs that stick out like whatever who remembers,
are those feet below me mine what face is this I have to look
    good
for the funeral somebody's, mine today

They're lying sweltering in their odour hell what perished here
    last night
what am I doing in this bed that keeps on moving who's that
    body here
beside me, they are saying this is rough hold on I'm falling
    through the universe
again this bed is slipping into space what is that figure on the
    carpet,
that's no painting that's my husband that's my wife I think I'm
    married
Who are you where am I now how did we meet o god not you

They're making whoopee in the barrel that is going over Bridal
    Falls,
Niagara, Wollomombi, Apsley Cataract, a dog a snake a wildcat
getting friendly as they tumble into mateyness and once again
    with feeling
to the top, here's Mister Sisyphus he's going up again
the warrior scuttling up the heights to that lone pine
that's every morning in the bedrooms of Australia

Michael Sharkey

Trophy Getters

Me and the young guys cough how women
flirt crude just like us.
We are the few who *get* them,
that's our boasting.
We know they want to love us heartfully
but have hard bargains from which we shy.
We call one over like an interview –
her of us as much as us of her.
'Far too homely,' we smirk
into our laughing-gas drinks.
'She'll make someone a nice first wife.'
Wife's not the point, we jibe:
tonight we're trifling from behind our Marlboros.
She is a form of money. We four would divvy her
if we were kinked that way.
The most neon our eyes can be,
the most muscled our smiles,
must lever her into decision:
is she Brad's tonight or mine?
Richo's or Hobbsy's?
The air blind and deaf with indoor night
and tom-tom bourbon.
My tactic, being older, is to offer her my seat,
bow too politely to be genuine,
and wish there were no laws to this,
that I could rip and lick right now
without remorse or evidence or bruise.

Craig Sherborne

Humility

For months Mozart has been so crucial I haven't played him.
The winds, filibustering the house, have heard
the chimney crackle and the paint strain
while the old obsessions went ignored. What was the point?
One evening I flipped the LP of the A major (K.488)
and the slow movement lacerated my defences
all over again. I squinted beyond the buddleia
on the fenceline and thought I could discern vast citadels
circling the horizon, and it was almost a joy
that swept its andante through the sad molecules
of my imaginings – but just then
a magpie alighted on the lawn, dragging a shadow
behind it as the sky turned a molten gold and a storm
broke from the west. The disc had ended
(I had no recollection of having heard the rondo finale)
and I sprang to the phone, jangling churlishly
to tell me you were gone. Music is like that:
it knows. It brought to mind what you had shown me
on the Baltic coast under the lighthouse:
twirling a miniature sailboat of souvenir amber
between thumb and forefinger, you pointed to the tower
and the encircling gulls and 'Look at them,' you said.
'They love the lighthouse. It teaches them the humility of flight.'

Alex Skovron

Murder at the Poetry Conference

The old pesticide factory
casts a buzz-saw shadow
on the wall of the council chambers.
Inside, the poets sit like aldermen.
They talk of war and genocide,
harrowing themselves silly.
At night they retire to soft floral sheets, flocked wallpaper.
   They dream
infinite shelves of books with tilted spines –
M and N shapes staggering away;
leather the colour of blood.

Melinda Smith

Where's my Rattan Overcoat?

where's my rattan overcoat? i have
things to say tonight at the basket
weaver's AGM! how find anything
for that matter in this dish of haste!
i never thought my collection of toothpicks
could take up so much room! where's
my snail shell rimmed spectacles
my echidna gloves! maybe i should
resume my search at high tide!
can i find my snakeskin snorkel!
here's my sunglasses made of smoke
now that's a find even though summer
is over & glaring at someone else
burning the edge of their rock pile

Pete Spence

The Knowledge

That he who distributes charcoal during a snowstorm
      is a fine fellow, and that to be
like a tree which covers with blossom the hand that shakes it
      warrants careful attention, and that
ice will not lodge on a busy spinning wheel –
      all this is common ground. Also,
to strike at the stars with a bamboo pole is the same
      as to dress in brocade and stroll in the dark,
or to offer a twenty-one-gun salute when the general
      has clapped spurs in his horse and departed.

And yes, pride is a flower from the devil's garden,
      and a well-groomed heart is a good match
for any well-groomed head. Repentance, they say,
      is the loveliest virtue, at least for a while:
and is it not odd that marriage is an assembly
      of strangers, and love an inscrutable monster?
My cousin has bought a farm and I have heartburn:
      but still, with my couple of loaves, I remember
to sell one and buy a lily and, nibbling
      a bamboo shoot, to bless its grower.

One hair on a pretty woman's head is enough
       to tether an elephant, but it's the creatures
that swag the knowledge home, as that the sunstruck
       ox pants at the sight of the moon,
that there's one phoenix to every thousand chickens,
       that a wren trying to walk like a stork
will break his crotch, that business is best done
       slow and steady as the cow slobbers.
No end of wisdom: but what does a frog
       in a well know of the waiting ocean?

Peter Steele

Bondi rock pool. 1963.

a line across a plane
a city marked in water and eucalyptus
an efficient takeover
a funnel web enters a sock

and at the edge of sea bondi's child
all hands and tongue sand in mouth
gathers the movement
of starfish and snails anemone and cuttle

an observer, unable to utter, takes place
a voice, silently present, observes
this child etched in salt and breath,
the child thrown up onto the shore,
the nets thrashing with slow death and light.

Amanda Stewart

Christmas Poem

Last Christmas
Your father did his impression
Of a Chinese person
Your mother wore a see-through dress
And served up salad
Made of grated carrot and sultanas
Your brother gave us tickets
To the monster trucks
Then his allergic children
Who were high on cordial
Knocked a bottle of red wine
Into my lap
Everybody laughed and said:
'What are you going to do, Adrian?'
'Go and write a poem about it?'

Adrian Stirling

The Ashes

The pig propped his hooves on the seat back and lifted the beer to his mouth. His toes, he saw over the translucent lip of the plastic cup, were perfectly clean if mottled in colour like the earth. The baying and howling intensified, and he turned his attention to the pitch. The raccoon dealt with the first ball, tossed hard in the lull following the crowd's jeering. The ball rolled dead. A rat retrieved it, spat on the red skin and briskly rubbed it on the hairless skin of his groin. The next ball curved like the smell drifting from rot, and the racoon was out. Plastic cups flew up into the sky and down again like scuttled locusts. It had happened so quickly. As the pig watched the racoon remove his helmet and return to the pavilion, he was momentarily unsettled. How fragile things seemed. How would they fill out the afternoon? The game, though, soon became robust and quite ordinary. The pig might have dozed off, for time passed. When he woke there was a commotion beneath his grandstand. The pig looked down into the bay. An old emu lay on its back in a concrete aisle littered with plastic cups, cigarette butts, pie bags and piss stains. Two paramedics, grey wolves, knelt over him. One had its paws buried in the oily feathers on the emu's upturned and distended chest. The bird's legs hung from each side like snapped sticks. There was a small and miscellaneous crowd. Then from the other side of the arena, with a great wailing and roaring, came another wave of plastic cups, catching the sun, hovering and shimmering like angels. The partnership on the field had been broken. The pig found himself hurling his own empty cup into the teeming oval of the sky. When the pig finally looked down at the aisle below, one of the wolves, its fur hoary as the grubby cement, had fetched a stretcher. Only the pig saw the wolves carry the large dead bird away.

Maria Takolander

After

After the silent removal
after the silt in the drain
after all that you'd hoped for
deftly excised from your brain
after the cat's been looked after
and the dog euthanised and the girl
who fed it on biscuits and munchies
quietly removed in a van
and after the garden is watered
and after the Rates are all paid
and after the roof is repaired
and the guy who's been screwing the maid
and the maid make a suitable marriage
and their kids have all fled from the land
and after the land has been conquered
by carbon dioxide and drought
and the unions are running the government
beyond a shadow of doubt
and the price of energy's rising
and the internet choking on smut
whose quality is as depressing
as the Stock Exchange in full rout
there will rise from the desert a something
we'd be probably better without
which will amble off into the cosmos
and turn the lights out

Andrew Taylor

Cave d'Aristide

It is not the world which passes our long-legged, small table
outside the Cave d'Aristide where we have hoisted ourselves
to settle on the slightly too-high stools.

With my dark glasses and light air,
my T-shirt striped horizontally, the image I am striving for
is more *faux Français* than *vrai Palavasien*.

Irony! Somehow this village condones its ease.
No, it's not 'the world', certainly not as literal
translation, but it's more than fellow-tourists,

who are few despite the excellence
of the picpoul de pinet, the beach, the sunlight,
the exchange rate and the mussels.

This spot, right on the corner
of Rue Aristide Briand,
is perfect for remembering his victims:

Paul Boible, railway worker, before the court
in 1910 for carrying a prohibited weapon,
to wit a corkscrew, the thousands

who tore up their mobilisation orders
and mailed the scraps to Aristide, the Paris sparkies
done out of their jobs by soldiers.

Ah, Aristide, it was Emma Goldman
who countered your scream of 'sabotage' with,
'Who but the most ordinary philistine will call that a crime?'

If there was a wine bar on some Rue Emma Goldman
somewhere, I'd be drinking there with the *cheminots*,
and Paul Boible would pull my cork.

But for now it's Aristide, and the sun sets
as the shopkeepers' kids play in the street
and I turn to my Mas de Daumas Gassac '06

and ask myself how ordinary a philistine I am.
Aristide, you were the prototype
for Chifley, Blair, all the Social Democrats

who (let's be kind) spun themselves into
contradiction. Were you, were any of them
aware of this? Here, on my stool,

(no armchair Marxist!) I can contemplate
not just the passing 'life', not just the wine,
but how my hedonism and my history

have put me here, my feet just off the pavement,
glad of not having to strike for five francs a day
and with the luxury of pretending to pretension.

Tim Thorne

Ambulance thinking

If the wail that whips around the valley
continues north, past the headland
the village mothers cross themselves
their broods safely south, they think.

Today a hopeful, hopeless rock fisherman
is washed into the greedy sea, or else
a holidaying tycoon has popped
an artery on the sodden golf-course –

their companions invoke
the snaking needle of sound, drawing in
the red flashing lights and the grim referees
already poised to call the game.

Helen Thurloe

Adventure at Sadies

Down the rabbit hole, we find
a world of cottage cheese and over-inflated
princedoms. That joke was thirty years too late.
Sitting there on the piazza
between the banana trees and austere flamingos,
we conjecture convivially on the poet's last fuck –
ing stand. He's got beautiful cheeks,
        beautiful eyes,
                beautiful thighs. And yet, he still
couldn't rate with a tardis. Between anthropomorphic stars
and unfamiliar history, a garden gnome quartet
practises dub karaoke and pert variety singers
live high in the grass. What price Russian formalism?
How unusual can an everyday poem be? These things,
wrestled with a knife and fork, remember Jameson.
We take what crumbs that sparrows throw us
and discuss the code of the West:
            common sense, Coalcliff, occasionally Coltrane.
That night you had the illness poem real bad,
coughed your guts up and took inclement gigabytes,
washed down with lachrymose love-notes from Spicer.
                  Hyperventilate now!, you said,
I can't find my postoffice. Was it a postoffice,
or just a plain old pawnshop? Sometimes we just
don't get history, or history doesn't get us. Say, haven't I
heard that before? Circularity breeds
stove-top despair, the coffee always spills twice.
Say hello to muffin-tops, good morning high-quality buns,
these baked goods so leavenly cool.
Oscar remonstrates with Shklovsky and finds a
substitute in Ken Brown: what a gambler!

And as we drive back south, we become
    part of the Great Tradition. Thanks Mum, thanks Dad,
        thanks Pam, Ken, Laurie, and the whole damn gang –
Rae, Denis, Tom, Barbara, Micky, Kelen, Alan, Erica,
           Kate, Leigh, Sal, and Kurt. (Ella, make a note!)

In the distance, someone waves, a touch sad.
          Athol don't be blue, be a marine aid,
          and watch over the incessant bridal parties,
          still caught in baby's breath and the last sure spray
              of the twentieth century.

Ann Vickery

View

It is worth knowing a fever at 38, so far.
Catching the calls of the boss beckoning from streets
all the way down. Sniff him out. Down some street, again.
Yellow chairs and new fruit. Winter knows nothing.

No crater
for 39 degrees, and shifting, for want of sweat.
Hvolsvelli, Britain. Marriage. Weddings and
the listless absent. Too hot even to touch bride,
even to touch groom. Better to be 39 and a half
losing sleep if winter is to be left to the previous
three months and we are to learn the trails of
longer walks. Smoke like mist for months.
No ash for days. Made it up from the blanket lounge.
Ate found cheese at the left fire. Late Pound trees
of the cleft liar. Date-mound knees draped with bereft
attire. Good company to be having, fishermen far off
enough that we eat their catch and hardly seen as they board
towering blue waves. Success. Coast, off the coast.
Off the coast, to the coast, to return by skeins. 40.
To be 40. Lining the river with college canoes. Better
yet, honest pumice soil. Sinking by the feet. 41. One
more down. Eventually, it will be hot enough to start something.

Corey Wakeling

The Piano Inkpot

We're scribbles at the margin of
nothing: that is to say
the edges of a sound-bite's edge,
altogether unreal as time
itself. The self that isn't there,

but when we hear a playing of
Chopin's miraculous ballades
we're not so little, nor so mean,
teetering on the fringe of space.
Our clock has been turned over, and

this music entertains the spheres,
as Shakespeare or Donne would have said
from quite another dispensation,
yet both had a hunch that we could be
only the tennis-balls of the stars.

Chris Wallace-Crabbe

Missing Miss Moore

Particularly adoring of wisteria
      Tiffany invented the system
of steel cables over lawns
from which their pendulous purples devolved
      like inverted tightrope walkers.
Matching lead to glass, he would say
Art is man's nature; nature is God's art
      which could have suited Miss Moore
      who might space it thus:
      Art is man's nature; nature
                is God's art
      from which beginning
             she would leap
             over skyscrapers of obstacles
and fly down tangents
      into luminous observations
            and curious obdurate facts
such as whether macaws shed tears
or cranes stand on one leg
      longer than a child ever could.
How we miss her and these facts
      carried out like a tray of glasses
      from the *Scientific American*
to us at the poolside sunlit page.

How we miss her frank primness,
Since no one has replaced
    this princess of praxis
        this patron of exemplars
          this sterling silver
scissors and paste adept who would, on discovering, say
        the prodigious word
    psilanthropism, show no fear
and blithely proceed to orchestrate the idea
    of Christ as mere male. Orchestration
    for light chamber orchestra
        was her fortepiano
    and we relished her scale passages
with their unexpected trills and tremolos and shakes.
        Who amongst us now
      can still remember
    those days of favourable Faber weather
    when Managing Director Captain Editor Eliot
      was flying the Union Jack
    and steering the ship amongst chthonic seas?
Who amongst us remembering
    that paper and that font
    and that generous severity
  will not regret those dappled waters,
      the outrunning tide
in which she proposed shallow sunlit sandwaves,
    little platforms, atolls and lily pads
      round which cephalopods
      (molluscs with tentacled heads)
    and ctenoids (fish with comb-like scales)
happily lap or paddle
    amongst Japanese paper flowers?

And just as scents cannot be recalled
the way visual memory floods,
and the overwhelming perfume of wisteria at dusk
cannot be remembered,
so no one has replaced or revived
the acute licorice tinctures
and memorable vanilla windows of Miss Moore.

John Watson

Happiness

Yes, I walked from Room 3
and down across the small bridge,
saw fingerlings there,
and along the harbour's curve
to its chrome edge,
a woman is laughing and telling
a story about her funny friends;
everything that happens to them
is so funny, and then the way
they tell the story; it is so funny;
I find her rather sad.
She is manning her stall
like a seagull, no one wants
to buy what she has; she wants
them to. She fusses over stall space.
A Jungian bus trip descends,
one of them my mother's stand-in.
I sit to write a letter, to organise
my thoughts, to withdraw
from contention, to close the practice.
I mention the absinthe sea
and liken the posting, the gift of it,
the perversity of a message in a bottle
being addressed to someone.
A Tasmanian waterfall in the top
right corner, twice. Surplus, five cent
platypuses in my coin purse,
bound for an international post,
float like displacement.

Meredith Wattison

Freely and with the appropriate sense of space

Dreams: lived, dreamt and composed for Ken Bolton

1.
A loft on the US West Coast. Out of a window the sun sinks
into the Pacific whilst Charles Bukowski is reading in Catullian
mode. 'Hey Catullus, you cocksucker!' he emotes. I tell him he
is a fraud but an amiable fraud. He replies that no one has ever
spoken to him like that and thus he respects me.

2.
Peter Skrzynecki is digging in his backyard. It is an overcast
day. His neighbour Judith Beveridge is looking over the fence.
Peter glances up. 'Hey Judith,' he asks, 'you dig?' Thinking this
some kind of innuendo Judith announces she is going to call
the police. They never arrive. Peter keeps digging.

3.
I am in a Chinese restaurant with Geoff Page, Alan Gould,
Les Murray and an Anglican bishop (in mufti) who has written
a life of Harold Holt. Murray and I sit next to each other, both
ordering a 'Num Duck'. A lot of the conversation is about
Harold Holt. I consider telling them about the weird sequence
on the former PM written by my one time student Jason Gunst
(which was nothing like the Holt I recall!) but instead tell them
of Monash student Mick Cahill telling me in 1968 'Ahh they
were on acid. I know some of that crowd and they were all on
acid.' Then Murray stands up, tells some kind of gag and does
a strange little dance.

4.
Geoff Eggleston and Shelton Lea are elected Labor members
of the Federal Parliament, and although both are deceased
no one seems to mind. Geoff is content to be a humble
backbencher but Shelley's ambitions are stymied by the PM,
who tells him that because of his rather colourful past he won't
obtain a ministry. Still, they are willing to offer him the post
of Speaker. 'That'll do me, brother,' says Shelley. The Liberal
members are a bit bewildered by Speaker Lea though the
Nationals are seduced by his rough hewn charm.

5.
A nightmare. I am on a plane, daylight outside. All is quiet,
very quiet. As if in preparation for an exam every passenger
is reading the same Bryce Courtenay novel.

6.
John Forbes, Gig Ryan and I are in what must be a thirties
screwball comedy. John is pursuing Gig, Gig is replying with
many witty lines (none of which I can remember) whilst I am
in an Edward Everett Horton-style support. This dream is all
mood.

7. (*for Jodie Magee*)
At the age I am now I have become a barrister. It is my first
case and I am defending a man in Horsham who has allegedly
murdered his wife. Robert Richter QC is prosecuting and this
fills me with certain apprehension. I am also anxious about the
questions I will ask and how I shall address the jury. At some
stage I get into an innocuous conversation about Horsham
with a rather dowdy female jury member, later thinking 'I
shouldn't have done that, I hope no one finds out.' But my
biggest worry centres on combining the careers of poetry and
the law. Then an answer to this problem arrives in the person
of Robert Richter. 'Welcome to the bar my learned friend,' he

says. 'I'm glad you're here because I've just started writing poetry and I'd love your opinion on what I've written.'

8.
I am in Lisbon. It is night and I am walking around with Alvaro de Campos who is raving in Scots accented English. Eventually I get to ask him 'What's it like being a heteronym?' He replies that *he* isn't a heteronym, the heteronyms are Albert Caeiro, Riccardo Reis and Fernando Pessoa, and that he, de Campos, invented them. Since he has spent time in Glasgow I ask him his opinion of Robbie Burns. I am told that Burns too is one of his heteronyms.

9.
The houses are a brilliant white, the sky an even more brilliant blue and Pi O is an exuberant village barber, forever singing. The villagers get him to compose songs for their weddings and he does though he won't attend the services which are run by his arch-enemy the village priest. Neither of them will walk on the same side of the street. End of dream.

10.
The early seventies. Allen Ginsberg and Lawrence Ferlinghetti are invited to tour Down Under but forgo the experience. Then some very enterprising literary entrepreneur achieves what one newspaper describes as 'What once was thought impossible': bringing Dante Gabriel Rosetti and Algernon Charles Swinburne to Australia. Rosetti, a quiet, gloomy man suffers from jet lag the entire time leaving the running to his colleague. And Swinburne in his green velvet suit and big red afro is an enormous hit: Bob Adamson and Vicki Viidikas meet him at Sydney Airport, sceptics like Nigel Roberts and Laurie Duggan are won over and of course the Tranters have him round for dinner. Then in Melbourne things get even more frantic. A sell out at La Mama has a massive crowd

clamouring well into Faraday Street. With a near carnival
ensuing the police block off Faraday at Lygon and Drummond.
Emboldened Swinburne climbs onto the back of a truck
and gives forth with some of his greatest hits. 'Come down
and redeem us from virtue,/Our Lady of Pain,' he declaims.
And in spite of, or because of him sounding very much like
bad imitation Dylan his audience is in positive uproar. The
Pre-Raphaelite revival is on and Australian poetry will never
be the same.

11.

The 1950s. The lamps are down low in a large London living
room for a meeting of 'The Room' a collection of poets some-
what like 'The Movement' and 'The Group'. In the garb and
accoutrements of the day (pipes, ties, elbow patches etc) they
are all very earnest young men except for one very earnest
young woman. One of their number reads a poem which I
gather is in praise of Mantovani, this being greeted with slow
smiles. Then another tells the young woman that he is going
to make a risqué comment. She nods and although I don't
quite hear the comment I see her smiling. How young and
earnest they are!

12

The mid seventies. Sir John Suckling and the Earl of Rochester
are both hip high school teachers: Suckling laid back in Phys.
Ed and Rochester perpetually stoned in Art. Rochester gets
upbraided by the principal for making a joke about Suckling's
surname which has resulted in the Phys. Ed teacher being called
Mr Blowjob throughout the school. Suckling though takes a
'Yeah man well whatever …' attitude. Rochester also gets into
a certain trouble by taking nude photos of Year 12 girls and
boys. A decade or so later dying of AIDS he is received into the
evangelical outreaches of Christendom by the Rev. Fred Nile.

Two decades on from that his photos mysteriously appear on
the Web.

13.
George Herbert is a well meaning sixties suburban vicar
who runs a Youth Fellowship following Sunday Evensong.
Contemporary folk music is played and although this
sometimes bewilders Rev. Herbert he still tries enjoying it.
The kids love him and call him Herbie. When a smart alec
interloper tries interrupting the vicar with stand up comedy
lines à la Bob Newhart or Shelley Berman the kids become
quite vehement: 'You leave Herbie alone!'

14.
Ivor Indyk and I are taking Alexander Pope on a tour of the
Sydney Writers' Festival, which in this case is a kind of side-
show alley. Pope is smallish, though not the misshapen midget
I've read about and this slightly bewilders me. Nevertheless I
have a feeling of trust about the man, if not the situation as
the Sydney Writers' Festival have not invited Pope and thus
he is our special, secret guest. My apprehension remains and
increases as I try recalling, but can't, Pope quotations that
I could recite to the great man. When Pope is distracted by
what appears to be a poetry slam in a large tent (and this
too is an embarrassment) I confide my anxieties to Ivor who
reassures me that Pope hasn't come all this way in time and
space just to hear his own words, and as for poetry slams well
the author of 'The Dunciad' can accommodate anything! And
it seems he can. Coming back from the slam tent Pope has a
large grin, ear-to-ear.

Alan Wearne

Poolside Reflections

The fact ... [the philosophers] constantly disagree with each other is
sufficient proof that they do not know the truth about anything.
    —DESIDERIUS ERASMUS, *The Praise of Folly (1509)*

Imagine my astonishment
to find a grey nurse shark
at least twenty kilometres from the sea
in my backyard swimming pool.

Too big to do laps, strictly speaking.
it circled while I looked on in fascination,
its dorsal fin parting the air
like the keel of a capsized boat
trapped in some endless eddy, which,
it struck me, could be a symbol of predestination –
of God's immutable and infallible power
guiding all things by necessity,
so that our will is in bondage to him
as Martin Luther expounded
in *De Servo Arbitrio.*

Except there was no eddy,
only a circular flow of water
drawn by the shark's own movement,
which, l reflected, could well be a symbol
of freedom of the will,
a concept defended by Erasmus of Rotterdam
in *De Libero Arbitrio*
who reasoned, to deny this
would make God responsible
for the sins of the world, which is
clearly inconsistent with his righteousness.

The finest minds of their age unquestioning
in their belief that God is the universal moral force
and man his moral creation,
yet reaching conclusions in contradiction.
How pleasing it was to realise
this great sunken Reformation controversy
had re-surfaced in my pool.

There remains, however, the question of the shark.

Ron Wilkins

The Stations of the Stairs

Beneath the new stairs
that rise from the beach,
the shallow cries or calls of children
and the floating lovers,
the old remain blurred
and bowed, instantly acquiring
an archaeological air.
These constructions
rise in stages like Apollo
with platforms for viewing
or resting, the salt
prickling at your back
arriving at last at a higher
if less sanctified place.

Warrick Wynne

A Line from Paracelsus

They exchanged few
words. He: *black sand,*
sea turtles, salt. Moist
shady areas. She: *the*

tree potentially contains
the pear. Different
combinations of lights
informed the etiquette.

The sign outside is
small, in English & He-
brew. Closed Saturdays.
It's an observant shop.

Mark Young

Publication Details

Robert Adamson's 'The Sibyl's Avenue' appeared in the *Age*, 21 August 2010.

Ali Alizadeh's 'Public Mourning' appeared in the *Age*, 20 November 2010.

Chris Andrews's 'Function Centre' appeared in *Blast* 12, Summer 2010.

Ken Bolton's 'The Funnies' appeared in *Steamer*, August 2011.

Ken Bolton and **John Jenkins**'s 'Volatile Condensate' will appear in their collection *Lucky For Some* (Little Esther Books, 2011).

Kevin Brophy's 'The Sublime' appeared in *Australian Book Review*, No. 332, June 2011.

Pam Brown's 'In my phone' appeared as the title poem in the pamphlet 'In my phone', *Wagtail* 111, June 2011.

joanne burns's 'tick' appeared in the *Age*, 23 October 2010.

Grant Caldwell's 'the lights are on' appeared in the *Age*, 4 September 2010; and his collection *glass clouds* (Five Island Press, 2010).

John Carey's 'on empty' appeared in *Quadrant*, July–August 2010.

Bonny Cassidy's 'Magma' will appear in *Young Poets: An Australian Anthology* (John Leonard Press, 2011).

Julie Chevalier's 'ms marbig No. 26 16' will appear in her collection *linen tough as history* (Puncher & Wattman, 2011).

Justin Clemens's 'We begin building that which cannot collapse because it will have to have been built as if it had already fallen' appeared in his chapbook *Me 'n' me trumpet* (Vagabond, 2011).

Sue Clennell's 'Picasso' will appear in *Indigo*, Summer 2011.

Jennifer Compton's 'Four Lines by Ezra Pound' appeared in *Quadrant*, September 2011.

Michael Crane's 'Metamorphosis' appeared in *Quadrant*, June 2011.

Bruce Dawe's 'Mini-series' appeared in the *Weekend Australian Review*, 5 March 2011.

Suzanne Edgar's 'Homage to Mapplethorpe' will appear in *Antipodes*, December 2011.

Brook Emery's 'You know the way' was published, in an earlier form, as part of the Blake Poetry Prize shortlist. (www.blakeprize.com.au)

Kate Fagan's 'Chrome Arrow' will appear in 'Fifty-one Contemporary Poets from Australia', *Jacket2* (online journal), October 2011. The source texts for 'Chrome Arrow' are Pam Brown, 'Laminex Radio', 'Darkenings', 'Evening', 'Blue Again', 'Miracles', 'Out and About', 'Blues in A', 'About a Death', 'Every American Wins a Prize', 'Augury', 'City Fringe', 'Thread Drift', 'Fall to Float' and 'Worldly Goods'; Alice Notley, 'It Would', 'Poem ("Why do I want to tell it")', 'Iphigenia', 'Mid-80's', 'Beginning with a stain, as the Universe did perhaps', 'At Night the States', 'Little Egypt' and 'How Spring Comes'; Emily Dickinson, Poems 1268, 321, 318 & 754; and Patti Smith, 'Witt', 'Translators (tr.)', 'Precious Little', 'Notice 2', 'Music (A Woman)' and 'The Pedestal'.

Diane Fahey's 'Terns' appeared in the *Canberra Times*, 26 February 2011.

Liam Ferney's 'Gli Ultimi Zombi' appeared in the *Age*, 26 March 2011.

Toby Fitch's 'Fluff' appeared on *The Red Room Company*, 2011. (www.redroomcompany.org)

Andrew Galan's 'The Suns Fall at Zero' appeared in *The Delinquent* (United Kingdom), Issue 14, April 2011.

Geoff Goodfellow's 'An Uncertain Future' appeared in his collection *Waltzing with Jack Dancer* (Wakefield Press, 2011).

Lisa Gorton's 'Dreams and Artefacts' appeared in *Australian Book Review*, No. 329, March 2011.

Robert Gray's 'Flying Foxes' appeared in *That's it, for now, HEAT* 24 new series, ed. Ivor Indyk (Giramondo, 2011).

Jennifer Harrison's 'Busker and Chihuahua, Chapel Street' appeared in the *Age*, 2 October 2010; and in her collection *Colombine: New and Selected Poems* (Black Pepper, 2010).

Jodie Hollander's 'The Humane Society' appeared in *Under the Radar*, January 2011.

Duncan Hose's 'The Truffle Hunters' appeared in *One Under Bacchus* (Inken Publisch, 2011).

D.J. Huppatz's 'FUTURE HAPPY BUDDHA vs Fake Kenny Rogers head' appeared in *VLAK – Contemporary poetics and the arts*, No. 2, 2011.

Mark William Jackson's 'The Frequency of God' appeared in *Windmills*, Fifth Edition, November 2010.

Evan Jones's 'Send in the Clowns' appeared in the *Age*, 23 April 2011.

Jill Jones's 'Break on Through' appeared in *The Diamond and the Thief*, June 2011.

Paul Kane's 'Triangulating the Tasman' appeared in *All Together Now: A Digital Bridge for Auckland and Sydney*, New Zealand Electronic Poetry Centre, 2010.

Cate Kennedy's 'Temporality' appeared in her collection *The Taste of River Water* (Scribe, 2011).

Richard King's 'Expat' appeared in the *Weekend Australian Review*, 11 September 2010.

Samuel Langer's 'into the index' appeared in *Otoliths* 21, 1 May 2011.

Geoffrey Lehmann's 'Unlicensed (from *Spring Forest*)' appeared in the *Sydney Morning Herald*, 4 December 2010.

Kate Lilley's 'Crush' appeared in the *Sun-Herald*, 12 June 2011.

Astrid Lorange's 'Lovetypes' appeared in her collection *Eating and Speaking* (Tea Party Republicans Press, 2011).

Anthony Lynch's 'Sonnet' appeared in the *Age*, 2 July 2011.

David McCooey's '(Weldon Kees)' appeared under a different title in the chapbook *Graphic*, 2010; and in the anthology *Outside* (Salt Publishing, 2011).

Jennifer Maiden's 'A Great Education' appeared in the *Age*, 15 January 2011.

John Miles's 'Snake Lady' appeared in the *Times Literary Supplement*, 26 November 2010.

Peter Minter's '*Claustrophilic Lavallière*' appeared in *All Together Now: A Digital Bridge for Auckland and Sydney*, New Zealand Electronic Poetry Centre. The quote at the head of the poem is from the poem 'Thoughts of a Young Girl' by John Ashbery (*The Tennis Court Oath*, Wesleyan University Press, 1962) and is used with permission.

Les Murray's 'Going to the City, Karachi 2010' appeared in *The Chimaera*, Issue 8, July 2011.

Nguyen Tien Hoang's 'Thursday April 21. Canberra' appeared in the *Age*, 23 July 2011.

Jal Nicholl's 'Values Meeting' appeared in the *Age*, 18 September 2010.

Mark O'Flynn's 'Our Lady of Coogee' appeared in *Page Seventeen*, Issue 8, November 2010.

Paul O'Loughlin's 'Reconfigured' appeared in *Zinewest*, October 2010.

Ouyang Yu's 'I love' appeared in *Landfall* (New Zealand), No. 221, 2011.

Louise Oxley's 'The Red Gurnard' appeared in the *Canberra Times*, 4 June 2011.

Geoff Page's 'A Manual of Style' appeared in *Extempore*, November 2010; and his collection *A Sudden Sentence in the Air: Jazz Poems by Geoff Page* (extempore, 2011).

Eddie Paterson's 'This is the only place' will appear in *Cordite* as a 'mixtape', December 2011.

Felicity Plunkett's 'Cyclone Plotting' appeared in *VLAK – Contemporary poetics and the arts*, No. 2, 2011.

Claire Potter's 'Misreading' appeared in *Jacket* 40, 2010.

David Prater's 'Cute' appeared in *Blackbox Manifold*, Issue 6, March 2011.

Peter Rose's 'Cicerone' appeared in the *Age*, 2 April 2011.

Penni Russon's 'Quote' appeared on her blog *Eglantine's Cake*, 2011. (www.eglantinescake.blogspot.com)

Gig Ryan's 'Daphnis and Chloe' appeared in her collection *New and Selected Poems* (Giramondo, 2011).

Andrew Sant's 'Mr Habitat Delivers a Speech to the Lapidarists' appeared in the *Age*, 12 February 2011.

Jaya Savige's 'January' appeared in *Jacket2*, September 2011.

Thomas Shapcott's 'Georges Perec in Brisbane' appeared in the *Weekend Australian*, 14 August 2010.

Michael Sharkey's 'Heroes of Australia' appeared in *Quadrant*, March 2011.

Alex Skovron's 'Humility' appeared in *Australian Book Review*, No. 329, March 2011.

Melinda Smith's 'Murder at the Poetry Conference' appeared in the *Canberra Times*, 26 February 2011.

Peter Steele's 'The Knowledge' appeared in his collection *The Gossip and the Wine* (John Leonard Press, 2010).

Amanda Stewart's 'Bondi rock pool. 1963.' was performed at the Australian Museum, Sydney, for the Sydney Consortium's 'Biodiversity and the Arts' event, 11 September 2010; and it will appear in *The Noise of Exchange*, Association of Stories in Macao, China, ASM Poetry, December 2011.

Ann Vickery's 'Adventure at Sadies' appeared in *Rabbit* 1, July 2011.

Corey Wakeling's 'View' appeared in the *Age*, 4 December 2010.

Chris Wallace-Crabbe's 'The Piano Inkpot' appeared in the *Age*, 5 February 2011.

Warrick Wynne's 'The Stations of the Stairs' appeared in *Eureka Street*, Vol. 21, No. 14, July 2011.

Mark Young's 'A line from Paracelsus' appeared in *E·ratio* 14, January 2011.

Notes on Contributors

THE EDITOR

John Tranter is the author of more than twenty books. His 2006 poetry collection *Urban Myths: 210 Poems: New and Selected* won multiple awards, including the Victorian, NSW and South Australian Premiers' Prizes. His latest book, *Starlight: 150 Poems*, in 2011 won the *Age* Book of the Year Award for Poetry and the Queensland Premier's Prize. (johntranter.com)

POETS

Robert Adamson is the author of many poetry volumes including *The Golden Bird* (Black Inc., 2008; C.J. Dennis Prize for Poetry 2009), and the editor of *The Best Australian Poems 2009* and *2010*. In 1995 he received the Christopher Brennan Award for lifetime achievement in poetry.

Ali Alizadeh's books include *Ashes in the Air* (UQP, 2011), *Evental* (Vagabond Press, 2011) and *Iran: My Grandfather* (Transit Lounge Publishing, 2010). He lives in Melbourne and teaches at Deakin University.

Richard James Allen is the author or editor of nine books. His work has been adapted for screen and has appeared widely in print and online. Dr Allen is an honorary associate to the University of Technology, Sydney in the creative practices area.

Chris Andrews has published a book of poems (*Cut Lunch*, Ginninderra Press, 2002) and translated books of fiction by Latin American authors, including César Aira's *Ghosts*. He teaches at the University of Western Sydney.

Jude Aquilina is an Adelaide Hills writer whose latest poetry collection, *WomanSpeak* (Wakefield Press, 2009), was co-written with Louise

Nicholas. She works at the SA Writers' Centre, teaches creative writing at the Adelaide College of the Arts and is Chair of Adelaide PEN.

Louis Armand lives in Prague. His recent books include a collection of poetry, *Letters from Ausland* (Vagabond Press, 2011) and a novel *Clair Obscur* (Equus, 2011). He is an editor of *VLAK* magazine.

Peter Bakowski's most recent poetry collection, *Beneath Our Armour* (Hunter Publishers, 2009), is comprised entirely of portrait poems of real and imagined people and is informed by two funded residencies in China.

Ken Bolton was born in Sydney in 1949. He works at the Australian Experimental Art Foundation in Adelaide and edits Little Esther Books. *A Whistled Bit Of Bop* (Vagabond Press, 2010) and *Sly Mongoose* (Puncher & Wattman, 2011) are recent collections.

Neil Boyack's stories and poems have been published in the collections *Black, Snakeskin-Vanilla, See Through* and *Transactions*. Neil is the creator and director of the *Newstead Short Story Tattoo*. (neilboyack.com)

Peter Boyle has published five books of poetry and translated three books of French and Spanish poetry. His most recent book, *Apocrypha* (Vagabond Press, 2009), won the Queensland Premier's Prize and the Arts ACT Judith Wright Prize and was shortlisted for the Australian Literary Society's Gold Medal.

Kevin Brophy teaches creative writing at the University of Melbourne. He is the author of eleven books, including four books of poetry. His latest poetry book is *Mr Wittgenstein's Lion* (Five Islands Press, 2007). He is patron of the Melbourne Poets Union and former editor of *Going Down Swinging*.

Pam Brown has published many books and chapbooks, and an ebook called *The meh of z z z z*. Her most recent title is *Authentic Local* (papertiger media, 2010). She lives in Alexandria, Sydney. (www.thedeletions. blogspot.com)

Joanne Burns is a Sydney poet. Her most recent book is *amphora* (Giramondo, 2011). She is currently working on a new collection, *brush*.

Michelle Cahill is a Goan-Anglo-Indian migrant writer who lives in Sydney. Her collections of poetry include *Vishvarūpa* (Five Islands

Press, 2011), shortlisted for the 2011 Alec Bolton Prize. She received the 2010 Val Vallis Award and the Inverawe Nature Poetry Prize (minor).

Grant Caldwell's latest collection of poetry is *glass clouds* (Five Islands Press, 2010). He is a lecturer in the creative writing program at the University of Melbourne.

John Carey is a Sydney poet, ex-teacher of French and Latin, and a former part-time actor. He has been published in *Meanjin*, *Quadrant* and *Southerly*, among others. His latest poetry collection is *The Old Humanists* (Puncher & Wattmann, 2008).

Bonny Cassidy is a Melbourne-based poet and writer. Her most recent collection is *Certain Fathoms* (Puncher & Wattmann, 2011). Bonny is currently undertaking the Marten Bequest Travelling Scholarship for poetry.

Julie Chevalier lives in Sydney. Two books of her poetry are forthcoming from Puncher & Wattman: *linen tough as history*, and *Darger: his girls*. A collection of short stories, *Permission to Lie*, was published by Spineless Wonders in 2011.

Justin Clemens's books of poetry include *Me 'n' me trumpet* (Vagabond Press, 2011). His latest book is a collection of art criticism, *Minimal Domination* (Surpllus, 2011); he is also co-editor of *The Jacqueline Rose Reader* (Duke, 2011) with Ben Naparstek. He teaches at the University of Melbourne.

Sue Clennell is the author of *The Ink Drinkers* and has recently released a poetry CD 'The Van Gogh Cafe'. She was placed in the 2006 and 2007 Josephine Ulrick Poetry Prize.

Jennifer Compton was born in New Zealand and now lives in Melbourne. Her book of poetry – *This City* (Otago University Press, 2011) – won the 2010 Kathleen Grattan Award in New Zealand. Her new play – *The Third Age* – was recently shortlisted for the Adam New Zealand Play Award.

Michael Crane's poetry collections include *A Dog Called Yesterday – Selected Poems and Prose* (Ninderry Press, 2003) and a chapbook, *Poems from the 29th Floor* (Picaro Press, 2007). He runs the Poetry Idol series at the Melbourne Writers' Festival and publishes the *Paradise Anthology*.

Fred Curtis is a Melbourne writer. His works include the booklet *Prosody: a Poetry Workshop* (Melbourne Poets Union, 2007). He holds a master's degree in creative writing from the University of Melbourne.

Toby Davidson is a West Australian poet who lectures in Australian literature at Macquarie University. He edited Francis Webb's *Collected Poems* (UWA Publishing, 2011) and his book *Born of Fire, Possessed by Darkness: Mysticism and Australian Poetry* is forthcoming from Cambria Press in 2012.

Bruce Dawe is the author of twenty books, including thirteen volumes of poetry. He was awarded the Order of Australia in 1992 for his contribution to Australian Literature. His latest book is *Slo-Mo Tsunami and Other Poems* (Puncher & Wattmann, 2011).

Sarah Day's most recent book is *Grass Notes* (Brandl & Schlesinger, 2009). Awards for her work include the Queensland Premier's Judith Wright Calanthe, the ACT Judith Wright, the University of Melbourne Wesley Michelle Wright Prize and the Anne Elder Award.

Suzanne Edgar's poetry collection *The Painted Lady* (Ginninderra Press, 2006) was shortlisted for the ACT's Best Book of the Year, 2007. Her forthcoming collection is *Talking Late*.

Brook Emery directed the Australian Poetry Festival in 2008 and 2010. Awards for his poetry include the Judith Wright Calanthe Prize for poetry, the Bruce Dawe National Poetry Prize and the Max Harris Award. His most recent collection is *Uncommon Light* (FIP, 2007).

Kate Fagan is a poet, editor and songwriter whose books include *The Long Moment* (Salt Publishing, 2002). A new collection, *First Light*, is forthcoming from Giramondo in 2012. Kate lectures in literature at the University of Western Sydney. (katefagan.com)

Diane Fahey's latest book is *The Wing Collection: New & Selected Poems* (Puncher & Wattmann, 2011). Her collection *Sea Wall and River Light* (Five Islands Press, 2006) won the ACT Judith Wright Poetry Award.

Jeltje Fanoy (jeltje) has authored collections including *Catching worms* (1993) and *Poetry Live in the House* (2004). She convened poetry performances at La Mama Poetica from 2004 until 2010 and is writing an account of her family's Dutch colonial experience.

Michael Farrell has written a Master's on the billycan in Australian poetry. His most recent publication is *thempark* (Book Thug, 2011). He is the current commentator on Australian poetry for *Jacket2*.

Johanna Featherstone is the founder and artistic director of The Red Room Company. Her most recent chapbook is *Felt* (Vagabond Press, 2010). She is a research associate with the University of Western Sydney.

Liam Ferney is a Brisbane poet. His most recent poetry collection is *Popular Mechanics* (Interactive Press, 2004). He has lived in the United States, South Korea and the United Kingdom.

Toby Fitch is an author and musician who was born in London and raised in Sydney. His poetry collections include the chapbook *Everyday Static* (Vagabond Press, 2010) and a forthcoming volume through Puncher & Wattman. (tobyfitch.blogspot.com)

William Fox is a Melbourne poet whose work has appeared in the *Age, Meanjin, Overland*, and various other print and online journals.

Andrew Galan has been published in *BLOCK, The Delinquent,* the *Eve's Harvest* anthology, *Streetcake, Verity La* and *REM Magazine.* He co-founded and runs Canberra poetry slam *BAD!SLAM!NO!BISCUIT!* at the Phoenix pub.

Angela Gardner is the author of two poetry collections: *Views of the Hudson* (Shearsman Books, 2009), written during a Churchill Fellowship visit to New York, and *Parts of Speech* (UQP, 2007), winner of the 2006 Arts Queensland Thomas Shapcott Poetry Prize. She is also a visual artist.

Carolyn Gerrish is a Sydney poet. She has published five collections of poetry. Her most recent is *The View from the Moon* (Island Press, 2011). She currently teaches creative writing at the WEA and is working on her sixth collection.

Jane Gibian's publications include her collection *Ardent* (Giramondo, 2007) and *small adjustments and other poems* (*Wagtail* poetry magazine, Picaro Press, 2008). Her work has been widely anthologised.

Geoff Goodfellow's latest collection is *Waltzing with Jack Dancer: a slow dance with cancer* (Wakefield Press, 2011). This is his tenth book, most of them going into multiple print runs. (geoffgoodfellow.com)

Lisa Gorton lives in Melbourne. Her first poetry collection, *Press Release* (Giramondo, 2007), won the Victorian Premier's Prize for Poetry. Her second poetry collection, *Hotel Hyperion*, is forthcoming from Giramondo in 2012.

Robert Gray is co-editor of the anthology *Australian Poetry Since 1788*. His *Collected Poems* will be appearing early next year.

Kathryn Hamann lives in Blackburn with her family. Her seventh collection is *A Slight Fuzzing of Perspective* (with photography by Leonard O'Brien and paintings by Sue Watson; Mono Unlimited, May 2011). (www.shardlight.com)

Jennifer Harrison's fifth poetry collection, *Colombine: New & Selected Poems* (Black Pepper, 2010), was shortlisted for the 2011 Western Australian Premier's Poetry Prize. In 2009 she co-edited the Puncher & Wattmann anthology *Motherlode: Australian Women's Poetry 1986–2008*.

Paul Hetherington's eight collections of poetry include *It Feels Like Disbelief* (Salt Publishing, 2007). His poetry awards include the 1996 ACT Book of the Year Award. He teaches at the University of Canberra and is a founding editor of the online journal *Axon: Creative Explorations*.

Sarah Holland-Batt was born in Queensland in 1982. Her first book, *Aria* (UQP), won the Arts ACT Judith Wright Poetry Prize, the Thomas Shapcott Poetry Prize, and the FAW Anne Elder Award. She lives in New York.

Jodie Hollander was raised in a family of classical musicians. Her poetry has been published in *Page Seventeen, Poetry Ireland, Under the Radar, Poetry New Zealand* and the *Warwick Review*, among others. She lives in Melbourne with her husband.

Duncan Hose is a poet, painter and academic scholar. His latest book of poems is *One Under Bacchus* (Inken Publisch, 2011). In 2010 he won the Newcastle Poetry Prize. (www.duncanhose.com)

D.J. Huppatz is a Melbourne-based writer who has published poetry in various journals both in Australia and the US. He also writes occasional literary criticism, and design and architectural criticism on his blog, *Critical Cities.*

Mark William Jackson was born in England in 1970. He now lives in Sydney with his wife and daughters. His work has appeared in various print and online journals including *Going Down Swinging.* Mark blogs on *Overland* and his own website. (markwmjackson.com)

John Jenkins is a Melbourne-based poet, writer and former journalist. His most recent book of poems is *Growing Up With Mr Menzies* (John Leonard Press, 2008) while his latest non-fiction book is *Travellers' Tales of Old Cuba* (Ocean Press, new edition, 2011).

A. Frances Johnson lectures in creative writing at the University of Melbourne. Her books include the novel *Eugene's Falls* (Arcadia, 2007), and she has a poetry collection, *The Wind-up Birdman of Moorabool Street*, forthcoming from Puncher & Wattmann.

Evan Jones was born in West Preston, Melbourne, in 1931. After studying journalism at the University of Melbourne, he spent the rest of his working life in academia until his early retirement in 1989.

Jill Jones has published six collections of poetry, most recently *Dark Bright Doors* (Wakefield Press, 2010), which was shortlisted for the 2011 Kenneth Slessor Prize. She is a member of the J.M. Coetzee Centre for Creative Practice at the University of Adelaide.

Paul Kane has published five collections of poems, most recently *The Scholar's Rock* (Otherland Publishing, 2011). He is poetry editor for *Antipodes.* He lives with his wife in Warwick, New York, with a second home near Talbot, in rural Victoria.

S.K. Kelen's poetry has been widely published for over thirty years. His collection *Earthly Delights* (Pandanus Books, 2006) was joint winner of the ACT's Judith Wright Award for a published book of poetry in 2007.

Cate Kennedy's three volumes of poetry are *Signs of Other Fires* (Five Islands Press, 2001), *Joyflight* (Interactive Publications, 2004) and *The Taste of River Water* (Scribe, 2011). She has won the Vincent Buckley Poetry Prize and the 2011 Victorian Premier's Literary Award for Poetry. She lives on a farm in north-east Victoria.

Richard King is a freelance writer. He writes regularly for the *Australian* and the *Sydney Morning Herald* and has been published in many magazines and journals. He lives in Fremantle, Western Australia. (richardjking.blogspot.com)

Graeme Kinross-Smith, an Honorary Fellow in Arts at Deakin University, is a poet, novelist, award-winning short fiction writer and photographer. His latest collection of poetry, *Available Light*, will appear shortly from Whitmore Press.

Andy Kissane's most recent collection, *Out to Lunch* (Puncher & Wattmann, 2009), was shortlisted for the NSW Premier's Kenneth Slessor Prize. A book of short stories, *The Swarm*, will be published in 2012. (andykissane.com)

Mike Ladd lives in Adelaide and produces *Poetica* on ABC Radio National. He has published six books of poetry and is currently working on a collection of short-form poems called *Miniatures*.

Sam Langer was born in 1983. His poems have appeared in the *Age*, *Otoliths* and *Overland*. He is the founding editor of *Steamer*.

Martin Langford has published six books of poetry, including *The Human Project: New and Selected Poems* (Puncher & Wattmann, 2009). He lives on the northern outskirts of Sydney.

Anthony Lawrence's latest poetry collection, *Bark* (UQP 2008), was shortlisted for the *Age* Poetry Book of the Year Award and the Queensland Premier's Award. His book-length poem *The Welfare of My Enemy U* is forthcoming.

Geoffrey Lehmann has released seven poetry collections and a *Selected Poems* and *Collected Poems*. He has edited two anthologies of Australian comic verse, and co-edited (with Robert Gray) two previous anthologies of Australian poetry.

W.M. Lewis is a Brisbane-based poet and fiction writer, whose epic haiku and poems have appeared in *Cordite Poetry Review*.

Kate Lilley's *Versary* (Salt Publishing, 2002) won the Grace Leven Prize and was shortlisted for the NSW Premier's Awards. Her second collection, *Ladylike*, is forthcoming from Salt Publishing.

Debbie Lim lives in Sydney. She received the 2009 Arts ACT Rosemary Dobson Prize for an unpublished poem. A chapbook is forthcoming with Vagabond Press in 2012.

Helen Lindstrom, a writer and teacher, grew up in Melbourne and now lives in Adelaide. Her first collection of poetry, *Cold Comfort,* was published by Brand New Lino Press in 2009 and republished by Ginninderra Press in 2011.

Astrid Lorange is a PhD candidate, teacher, researcher, editor and poet from Sydney. Her poetry books include *Eating and Speaking* (Tea Party Republicans Press) and *Minor Dogs* (bas-books), both published in 2011.

Roberta Lowing's first book of poetry *Ruin* (Interactive Press, 2010) was joint winner of the 2011 Asher Literary Award. Her first novel *Notorious* (Allen & Unwin, 2010) was shortlisted for the 2011 Prime Minister's Literary Award and the 2011 Commonwealth Writers' Prize.

Anthony Lynch is an editor with Deakin University and the publisher for the independent poetry press, Whitmore Press. His first collection of poetry, *Night Train*, is about to appear from Melbourne publisher Clouds of Magellan.

David McCooey's first book of poems, *Blister Pack* (Salt Publishing, 2005), won the Mary Gilmore Award. His second collection, *Outside*, is forthcoming from Salt Publishing. He teaches literary studies and professional & creative writing at Deakin University, Victoria.

David McGuigan is a poet, town planner and teacher, recently returned to Adelaide from teaching students on remote Aboriginal communities. He has had many poems and short stories published in journals around Australia.

Rhyll McMaster's poetry has won awards including the C.J. Dennis and Grace Leven prizes. Her collection *Late Night Shopping* will be published in 2012 by Brandl & Schlesinger.

Jennifer Maiden was born in Penrith in 1949. Her many awards include the Christopher Brennan Award for Lifetime Achievement. Her latest collection, *Pirate Rain* (Giramondo, 2010), won the 2011 NSW Premier's Prize.

John Miles has published two books of poems and a new collection is nearing completion. His awards include winning the Shrewsbury International Poetry Competition.

Peter Minter is a leading Australian poet, editor and scholar. He is poetry editor of *Overland* magazine.

Les Murray's work has been published in ten languages. He has won many literary awards, including the T.S. Eliot Award (1996) and the 1999 Queen's Gold Medal for Poetry, on the recommendation of Ted Hughes.

David Musgrave is publisher at the independent press Puncher & Wattmann, which he founded in 2005. His four books of poetry include *Phantom Limb* (John Leonard Press, 2010), which won the Grace Leven Prize for Poetry in 2011.

Nguyen Tien Hoang arrived in Australia from Vietnam in 1974. His poems and essays have appeared widely, including in a published collection, *Beyond Sleep* (1990). He is on the editorial panel of literary e-magazine *damau.org*.

Jal Nicholl lives in Melbourne, where he writes and paints as much as time and work commitments allow.

Mark O'Flynn has published two novels as well as three collections of poetry, most recently *What Can Be Proven* (Interactive Publications, 2007). A third novel is forthcoming from HarperCollins. He lives in the Blue Mountains.

Ella O'Keefe is a PhD candidate at Deakin University in the School of Communication and Creative Arts. Her work includes radio pieces aired on Radio National. She currently lives in Melbourne.

Paul O'Loughlin is a Sydneysider who, with a number of poems in anthologies, in 2010 published his first collection of poetry.

Ouyang Yu, originally from China, has by the age of fifty-six published fifty-nine books. His latest English poetry collection is *The Kingsbury Tales* (Brandl & Schlesinger, 2008).

Louise Oxley has published two collections, *Compound Eye* (2003) and *Buoyancy* (2008), with Five Islands Press, and a selection of her work, *Sitting with Cézanne*, is Picaro Press's *Wagtail* 41.

Geoff Page is a Canberra-based poet. His latest books are *Agnostic Skies* (Five Island Press, 2006) and *60 Classic Australian Poems* (UNSW Press, 2009). He has also released a CD, *Coffee with Miles* (River Road Press, 2009).

Eddie Paterson's poems have been widely published. He is a lecturer in creative writing at the University of Melbourne.

Janette Pieloor's poetry has been published in magazines and journals. She was runner-up in 2009 for the ACT Michael Thwaites Poetry Award. She lives in Canberra and is currently working on her first collection of poetry.

Felicity Plunkett's first collection of poetry, *Vanishing Point* (UQP, 2009), won the Thomas Shapcott Prize and was shortlisted for the Western Australian Premier's Book Awards. Her latest chapbook is *Seastrands* (Vagabond Press, 2011). Since 2010 she has been poetry editor at UQP.

Claire Potter was born in Perth. In 2006 she was awarded an Australian Young Poets Fellowship. Her first full-length collection is *Swallow* (Five Islands Press, 2010).

David Prater was born in Dubbo in 1972. Papertiger Media published his first poetry collection, *We Will Disappear*, in 2007. Since 2001 he has been the managing editor of *Cordite Poetry Review*. He currently lives in Karlskrona, Sweden.

Aden Rolfe is a Melbourne-based writer whose work includes performance writing, collage and criticism. His poetry has appeared in *Overland*, *The Best Australian Poetry 2009* and the *Melbourne Historical Journal*.

Peter Rose is the author of a family memoir, *Rose Boys* (Allen & Unwin, 2001), which won the National Biography Award in 2003. His latest novel is *Roddy Parr* (Fourth Estate, 2010). His new poetry collection, *Crimson Crop*, will appear in early 2012. He is the editor of *Australian Book Review*.

Penni Russon lives in St Andrews with her husband and young children. Her most recent novel is *Only Ever Always* (Allen & Unwin, 2011). She maintains a blog called *Eglantine's Cake*.

Gig Ryan has been poetry editor at the *Age* since 1998. She has published eight collections of poetry, the most recent being *New and Selected Poems* (Giramondo, 2011).

Philip Salom's books include the satirical verse-novel *Keepers* (Puncher & Wattmann, 2010), the first of a trilogy. In 2003 he received the Christopher Brennan Award.

Andrew Sant jointly founded and edited for ten years the Tasmanian-based quarterly, *Island*. The most recent of his poetry collections is *Fuel* (Black Pepper, Melbourne, 2009). Born in London, he now lives in Melbourne.

Michael Sariban is a Brisbane-based poet whose work has appeared in a wide variety of Australian and overseas publications. His collections include *A Formula for Glass* (UQP, 1987) and *Luxuries* (Ginninderra Press, 2001).

Jaya Savige's debut poetry collection, *Latecomers*, won the NSW Premier's Kenneth Slessor Prize, the Arts Queensland Thomas Shapcott Prize and the Arts Queensland Val Vallis Award. His second volume is *Surface to Air* (UQP, 2011).

Mick Searles lives in Adelaide.

Thomas Shapcott was born in 1935. He is the author of many books of poetry, fiction (novels and short stories) and libretti. Most recent are the poetry collection *Parts of Us* (UQP, 2010) and the memoir *A Circle Around My Grandmother* (Papertiger, 2010).

Michael Sharkey's most recent book is *The Sweeping Plain* (Five Islands Press, 2007, reprinted 2011, Picaro Press). A new collection, *Another Fine Morning in Paradise* (Five Islands Press) is forthcoming in 2012.

Craig Sherborne's first poetry collection is *Bullion* (Penguin, 1995). His acclaimed memoir *Hoi Polloi* (Black Inc., 2005) was followed by *Muck* (Black Inc., 2007), winner of a Queensland Premier's Prize, and a novel, *The Amateur Science of Love* (Text Publishing, 2011).

Alex Skovron is the author of five poetry collections, most recently *Autographs* (Hybrid, 2008). Awards for his poetry include the Wesley Michel Wright Prize, the John Shaw Neilson Award and the *Australian Book Review* Poetry Prize. He lives in Melbourne and works as a freelance editor.

Melinda Smith is the author of *Pushing Thirty, Wearing Seventeen* (2001) and *Mapless in Underland* (2004), both published by Ginninderra Press. She has a collection of poems about autism coming out in April 2012. (www.melindasmith.wordpress.com)

Pete Spence was born in Ringwood, Victoria, in 1946. His first book was *5 Poems* (Nosukomo, 1986), and his most recent book is *Perrier Fever* (Grand Parade Poets, 2011). He is also a visual poet and a film-maker, and he now lives in Kyneton with his partner and their son.

Peter Steele, a Jesuit priest, was born in Perth but has spent most of his life in Melbourne. His most recent publication is *The Gossip and the Wine* (John Leonard Press, 2010).

Amanda Stewart is a poet, author and vocalist. Her book and CD set of selected poems, *I/T*, won the Anne Elder Poetry Prize. Her recent publications include the short play *Solace* (Beckett Pause, Sondersahl Press, Vienna, 2007).

Adrian Stirling was born in Geelong in 1977. He divides his time between teaching, writing and playing bass guitar. He has written two novels: *Broken Glass* (2008) and *The Comet Box* (2011).

Maria Takolander's first book of poems, *Ghostly Subjects* (Salt Publishing, 2009), was shortlisted for a 2010 Queensland Premier's Literary Award. She is a senior lecturer in literary studies and creative writing at Deakin University in Geelong.

Andrew Taylor's more than fifteen books of poetry include *The unhaunting* (Salt Publishing, 2009), which was shortlisted for the 2009 Western Australian Premier's Book Awards. He is professor emeritus at Edith Cowan University and divides his time between Perth and Wiesbaden in Germany.

Tim Thorne is the author of twelve collections of poetry, the most recent being *I Con: New and Selected Poems* (Salt Publishing, 2008). He established the Tasmanian Poetry Festival and was its director for seventeen years.

Helen Thurloe lives on Sydney's northern beaches. She has worked in politics, business and government. Her poetry has been included in the Poetica Christi anthology *Horizons* (2010).

Ann Vickery is a Monash Fellow in the Centre for Women's Studies and Gender Research at Monash University. Her books include *Stressing the Modern: Cultural Politics in Australian Women's Poetry* (Salt Publishing, 2007), which was shortlisted for a NSW Premier's Prize.

Corey Wakeling grew up in Perth and lives in Melbourne. His poetry has been widely published in Australia and abroad. He is a tutor and PhD candidate at the University of Melbourne.

Chris Wallace-Crabbe AO is professor emeritus of the Australian Centre, University of Melbourne, and chair of the Australian Poetry Centre. His latest collection is *Telling a Hawk from a Handsaw* (Manchester Carcanet Oxford Poets, 2008). He received the Order of Australia in 2011 for his service to the arts.

John Watson's books include *A First Reader* (Five Islands Press, 2003), *Erasure Traces* (Puncher & Wattmann, 2008), *River Syllabics* (Picaro Press, 2009) and *Four Refrains* (Picaro Press, 2011).

Meredith Wattison was born in 1963 and lives outside Sydney. She has published five books of poetry, the latest being *Basket of Sunlight* (Puncher & Wattman, 2007). *terra bravura* (Puncher & Wattmann) is due out in 2012.

Alan Wearne's next book will be *Cabin Crew, Prepare the Cabin for Landing* (Giramondo, 2012). He has recently established Grand Parade Poets, a publishing house.

Ron Wilkins is a Sydney scientist. His poetry has been published in *Blue Dog*, *Five Bells* and *Quadrant*, among others. His poetry volume, *Fistful of Dust*, is forthcoming.

Warrick Wynne is a Melbourne poet and teacher. His most recent collection is *The State of the Rivers and Streams* (Five Islands Press, 2002). (warrickwynne.org)

Mark Young has been publishing poetry for over fifty years. He is the author of more than twenty books, primarily poetry but also including speculative fiction and art history. He is the editor of the ezine *Otoliths*. He lives on the Tropic of Capricorn.